"For the person who is bereaved or otherwise experiencing loss or hurt, *Healing Takes Time* is written as a gentle companion—not a theoretical treatise or an instruction manual or a set of lectures or sermons, but as a pastoral encouragement and support. There is nothing intrusive about it. People who turn to it repeatedly over days and weeks will find solace and help, here from an anecdote, there from a carefully chosen quotation from Scripture; along the way a suggestion for prayer or a useful insight from the day's title or some refreshment simply from the repeated reminder to 'take some moments and rest with God.' Dr. Gallagher is a patient and gracious pastor in a time of great need."

*—John L. Hügel*
*Associate Professor of Biblical Studies*
*University of Sioux Falls, Sioux Falls, South Dakota*

"Because 'Healing Takes Time,' Dr. David Gallagher's deceptively brief devotional is all the more important as a companion along the way. For those who have experienced loss in any of its shattering and life-transforming manifestations, this book is a sensitive and encouraging guide. With a seasoned pastor's deep store of experiences and a fellow-sufferer's intimate knowledge of the terrain of grief, Dave shares his vignettes, drawn from his own life and from the losses of those he knows. With a word of Scripture, a brief prayer, and a suggestion or encouragement, he makes God's own concern palpable and real."

*—Dennis E. McFadden, President/CEO*
*Atherton Baptist Homes*

"Dr. Gallagher invites you on a journey of healing in *Healing Takes Time*. It is a practical guide, offering encouragement for the times when we feel so alone in our loss, offering hope that, in time, God heals our hurts—He is faithful! Jane Bruzzese, Program Director for Interfaith Community Care, comments, 'The vignettes, useful Scriptural encouragement, questions for self-reflection, practical-step suggestions, and prayers are relevant, sensitive, and helpful in providing guidance for the healing journey that takes time—with God's help and his healing touch.'"

*—Michelle Dionisio, President/CEO*
*Interfaith Community Care, Surprise, Arizona*

# Healing Takes Time

*David P. Gallagher*

**LITURGICAL PRESS**
Collegeville, Minnesota

www.litpress.org

Cover design by Bro. Joachim Rhoades, O.S.B. Photograph by Frederic Cirou, PhotoAlto.

1      2      3      4      5      6      7      8

**Library of Congress Cataloging-in-Publication Data**

Gallagher, David P.
   Healing takes time / David P. Gallagher.
      p.   cm.
   Summary: "A practical guide to spiritual and emotional healing through the author's personal reflections, Scripture quotations, practical steps, probing questions, list of resources, and ecumenical-Christian encouragement"—Provided by publisher.
    ISNB-13: 978-0-8146-1523-2 (pbk. : alk. paper)
    ISBN-10: 0-8146-1523-6 (pbk. : alk. paper)
   1. Suffering—Prayer-books and devotions—English   2. Suffering—Religious aspects—Christianity.   3. Loss (Psychology)—Religious aspects—Christianity.   4. Consolation.   5. Spiritual healing.   I. Title.
BV4909.G35   2005
242'.4—dc22                     2004030647

*This book is dedicated to those who have experienced
loss and need healing:*

*To our niece and her husband, Jennie and Duke Hoenig,
who lost their baby minutes after birth,
and to Jim and Jeannie Evans, parents and grandparents,
who were there to help, pray, guide, and encourage
during those difficult times.*

*To Kathy Felton, sister of our daughter-in-law,
who lost her four-day-old baby
and whose husband was tragically murdered,
now finding herself a single parent
with the responsibility of raising two very young children.*

*To the scores of members and friends
at Palm West Community Church
who have lost loved ones,
agonized over children and grand children's losses,
and yet have gained victory because of God's grace.*

*To all who have experienced loss
and have found themselves
on the journey of grief and healing:
My prayer is that this book will be a helpful guide
in your healing process and that you will be reminded
of God's sovereign love and grace,
remembering that healing takes time—lots of time.*

*Finally, this book is dedicated to those
who will experience loss in the days ahead,
with the prayer that you may find
strength and encouragement
by turning to Holy Scripture, friends,
and the God of hope and peace who brings final victory.*

# Acknowledgments

Most people realize that loss may hit suddenly, unexpectedly, and with devastating results. For years, I have wanted a simple, concise resource that I could put into the hands of someone moving through the grief process.

This book would never have been written without the encouragement of so many hurting people who, by their attitudes, responses, and actions, reminded me that healing takes time—lots of time. As a result, I prepared a simple collection of personal experiences and Scriptures that give strength and encouragement, and I asked what some colleagues and friends thought. I am particularly indebted to:

✦ Dr. Roy B. Zuck at Dallas Theological Seminary for his friendship, encouragement, and guidance throughout the preparation of this manuscript. Roy read and edited the manuscript at the beginning and has proved to be a true friend.

✦ Fr. Cyril Gorman, pastoral editor at Liturgical Press, for his continuous encouragement and insights suggesting the many personal practical stories from my own experiences.

✦ My wife, Mary Ann, who has gone with me hundreds of times to meet with people who are hurting and experiencing loss and who has been a faithful partner in ministry with me for over thirty-six years.

# Introduction

Experiencing loss offers a choice. We may choose to become a bitter person or we may choose to become a better person. This book is a practical biblical resource that can help you on your journey of healing. Time is a powerful ingredient to healing. Often we think the loss of a family member or friend is the greatest loss in life. Losing a loved one is devastating, but there are many other shattering experiences in life. Physical and mental challenges, drug abuse, or various dependencies are huge challenges.

You or someone you know may be newly wed, perhaps coping with infertility. The loss of an unborn child or the experience of sudden infant death syndrome is heartbreaking. Some people are entering or reentering the job market; others are thinking about or entering retirement. Some are dealing with adoption issues or are victims of crime. Survivors of natural disasters or other catastrophes need hope. Those serving in the military face loneliness, and people who are terminally ill or are caring for family or friends who are terminally ill are stressed beyond imagination.

Today many persons experience separation or divorce. Many persons are hospitalized, under hospice care, or convalescing. Some persons have become single parents. Others are experiencing vocational stresses, such as relocation, reorganization, termination, or starting a new job. Refugees and students living away from home face challenges. Loneliness, loss, and sorrow come on inmates in jails, prisons, and detention centers. Caregivers and parents present challenges, especially those whose children have attention deficit disorder or hyperactivity. Terrorist attacks, weapons of mass destruction, and world chaos have become normal words in our vocabulary. This book is intended to give you strength.

Most people have heard about the stages of grief: shock, denial, resentment and anger, and acceptance and readjustment.[1] It is one thing to read about the stages and understand them academically—in your mind. It is quite another thing to prayerfully walk through those stages step by step, day by day over a period of time. That's where this little book comes in. *Healing Takes Time* is a practical guide to help you through the journey of healing. This book can be used in a variety of ways: The fifty-two meditations and reflections offered here may be used weekly, monthly, or at your own pace. They may be used by yourself or with a friend. They may be used as a small group discussion starter for weeks or months to help you or your group in the journey of healing.

Each meditation provides (a) a theme, (b) some helpful Scripture, (c) a personal practical illustration from experience, (d) some practical steps to take, and (e) a space for you to journal (if you wish). You might use some of the lines on successive readings of the book. At the end of this book there is a special resource for times when you are feeling particularly in need as a special source of power and encouragement—times when you may feel desperate.

My prayer is that God will use this book to help you on your spiritual journey of healing.

And remember: healing takes time—lots of time.

---

[1] For a discussion about the stages of grief, see any of Elisabeth Kübler-Ross' books, for example, *Death: The Final Stage of Growth* (New York: Simon & Schuster, 1986); *On Death and Dying* (New York: Scribner Classics, 1997); or *Living with Death and Dying* (New York: Macmillan, 1981). These works are available in various editions and reprints.

# Meditations and Reflections

# Today with God's help: I will begin my healing journey with God

## Encouragement from experience

This book is for you. I wrote it because of my own journey and the journeys that I've seen others experience. This book is intended to be a resource for reading and reflecting, perhaps even daily, for strength, hope, and encouragement. Today you begin a journey with meditations that will give you hope from Scripture, the Bible, God's Word. As you begin, be reminded that just as everyone needs time to heal physically; everyone, including you, needs time to heal emotionally and spiritually. At the very start let us be thankful to God for the helps that come our way. I pray that this book may be one such help for you.

This book is arranged so that you can read each meditation, and then spend some time reflecting on a Scripture passage. At times, you may want to look up verses in the Bible. I accept the reality that God's promises offer me hope. Today, as you begin your spiritual journey of healing, trust God to strengthen you each new day. In the words that follow, you can imagine yourself as hearing or speaking the words: Sometimes the voice is mine. Sometimes the voice is yours. Sometimes the voice is God's.

## Encouragement from Scripture

"You will seek me and find me when you seek me with all your heart. I will be found by you," declares the LORD. (Jeremiah 29:13-14)

For no matter how many promises God has made, they are "Yes" in Christ. And so through him the "Amen" is spoken by us to the glory of God. (2 Corinthians 1:20)

*My response as I claim God's promises and grow stronger*

What healing work does God need to do in my life today? Have I told him about that need?

*Practical steps that I will take today*

Today I will be patient with myself and claim God's faithfulness. I will remember that healing takes time—lots of time.

*My prayer*

Lord, thank you for your faithfulness to me today.

*Now I will take some moments to rest with God.*

*My spiritual healing journal*

Date     Thoughts / Feelings / Insight Gained / Prayer

_____

_____

_____

_____

_____

# 2 Today with God's help: I will keep perspective and trust in God's faithfulness

*Encouragement from experience*

I was approaching my fortieth birthday. Thirty was a struggle for me but forty—no way. I wanted little done or said about my fortieth birthday. We had a small family dinner and some gifts were given. For me it was, "Let's get through this as quietly and quickly as possible." A very dear friend gave me a little gift. I didn't realize it at the time, but that little gift was very significant. In fact, it took me about ten years to realize its significance. It was a coffee mug with the words "Life Begins at 40" printed on it. You've seen them. Frankly, it was only out of politeness that I said thank you to her, for I really didn't like the thought of being forty, and I certainly was not going to use that little cup that would remind me every day that I was "over 40." So I quietly and unassumingly put the little cup on the top shelf of our kitchen cabinet (clear in the back). The little cup remained there for a long time, actually for many years. Without realizing it, a decade had passed. I was approaching fifty, but honestly, I still felt like I was twenty. After my birthday celebration was over and everyone left or went to bed, I remembered that little cup. I quietly strolled over to the kitchen and reached way back behind the other cups and found the "Life Begins at 40" cup. I looked at it through new eyes. I had learned a very important lesson about life itself. Perspective is important for anyone going through a difficult time, and perspective is often lost when we are in the midst of pain, loss, or suffering.

Perspective is an important word as we face challenges. Scripture tells us that God *is* faithful. We may not *feel* like God is faithful while we are in the midst of a storm, but our faith keeps us strong. In the Bible there are two basic principles: (1) The Bible affirms God's faithfulness. (2) God is faithful to me even during times when I do not feel God's faithfulness. God *is* there.

*Encouragement from Scripture*

Because of the LORD's great love we are not consumed, for his compassions never fail. They are new every morning; great is your faithfulness. I say to myself, "The LORD is my portion; therefore I will wait for him." (Lamentations 3:22-24)

Your steadfast love, O LORD, extends to the heavens,
   your faithfulness to the skies. (Psalm 36:5; NRSV)

*My response as I claim God's promises and grow stronger*

When has God shown his faithfulness in my life? How do I see God at work in my life today?

*Practical steps that I will take today*

Today I will begin to understand that healing may be slow, and I will take one day at a time. I will remember that healing takes time—lots of time.

*My prayer*

I claim your steadfast faithfulness for my life today and I give you thanks.

*Now I will take some moments to rest with God.*

*My spiritual healing journal*

Date        Thoughts / Feelings / Insight Gained / Prayer

_____

_____

_____

_____

_____

# 3 Today with God's help: I will reflect on aspects of God's faithfulness

*Encouragement from experience*

When I woke up this morning the sun was up and shining. I couldn't help but think of how good God is every day. I didn't worry about the sun coming up; I knew it would come up—it always does. Why? Because God is faithful. The rising sun reminded me of God's faithfulness. God's faithfulness is a continual theme in Scripture. God's faithfulness means that I have assurance of salvation and forgiveness (John 10:27-30; 1 John 1:9) and it assures me that he will provide me strength as I face loss, sorrow, loneliness, and affliction (1 Peter 4:12-13). It is important to remember that God's faithfulness means that I can have peace and victory (1 Corinthians 10:13) and that I have spiritual blessings from a sovereign God (1 Corinthians 1:9; Psalm 84:11-12). God's faithfulness also means that I can reflect God's love and grace in my life as I yield my life to him (Galatians 5:22-23).

*Encouragement from Scripture*

O LORD, you will hear the desire of the meek;
> you will strengthen their heart, you will incline your ear
to do justice for the orphan and the oppressed,
> so that those from earth may strike terror no more.
> (Psalm 10:17-18; NRSV)

*My response as I claim God's promises and grow stronger*

How has God shown divine faithfulness to me? How has God shown divine faithfulness to my family, at my job, or with material provisions?

*Practical steps that I will take today*

Today I will face my emotions and connect with other people who care. I will remember that healing takes time—lots of time.

*My prayer*

You are faithful, O God, and I love you. Help me to follow you!

*Now I will take some moments to rest with God.*

*My spiritual healing journal*

Date        Thoughts / Feelings / Insight Gained / Prayer

_____

_____

_____

_____

_____

# 4 Today with God's help: I will remember that burden bearing means sharing

*Encouragement from experience*

My father was critically ill. I was so thankful that a close friend of mine was there in the hospital room with me. My friend stood there with me at the bedside in the hospital room, but he remained totally quiet. After my father passed away, the two of us left the hospital room. My friend didn't say a word. We walked down the long hospital corridor; still no word was spoken. We stepped into the elevator in complete silence. Not one word was spoken even during the long walk out of the lobby across the parking lot to the car. My friend's arm was around me; I had just lost my father and no words would be appropriate. When we reached the car, the first words were spoken. I looked into the eyes of my friend and quietly whispered, "Thank you, my friend." Sometimes burden bearing is about sharing things other than words. Sometimes sharing feelings is even more important. Sometimes just being quiet and letting God speak is very important.

*Encouragement from Scripture*

> I waited patiently for the LORD;
>     he inclined to me and heard my cry. (Psalm 40:1; NRSV)

*My response as I claim God's promises and grow stronger*

Who can I go to who really cares and listens? Don't forget God!

*Practical steps that I will take today*

Today I will accept and rejoice over even the smallest step that I take by God's grace. My tears and the tears of friends will become a comfort to me. I will not be afraid because I will trust in God for strength today. I will remember that healing takes time—lots of time.

*My prayer*

Help me to share with not only you, God, but also with special people in my life.

*Now I will take some moments to rest with God.*

Date    Thoughts / Feelings / Insight Gained / Prayer

_____

_____

_____

_____

_____

## 5 Today with God's help: I will take a personal burden bearing inventory

*Encouragement from experience*

I was leading a funeral service one morning and my wife was seated toward the back, keeping an eye on a kindly gentleman she was aware of in our congregation; he had recently lost his wife. As I spoke, I saw my wife quietly get up and walk down the aisle to the grieving man. My wife knelt down on the floor near the grieving man and she wrapped her arms around him and stayed there until the service was over. We all need people who care—people who will be burden bearers with and for us.

Take a few minutes to reflect on and respond to the following: As I look closely at my life these days, what am I most concerned about? If I could change one thing about my life, what would I change? What does it mean to carry someone else's burden? Why is it helpful for me to share my struggles? With whom should I share my struggles?

*Encouragement from Scripture*

"Though the mountains be shaken and the hills be removed, yet my unfailing love for you will not be shaken nor my covenant of peace be removed," says the LORD, who has compassion on you. (Isaiah 54:10)

*My response as I claim God's promises and grow stronger*

How might I have allowed my own concerns to override my consideration for others? Who in my life could benefit from a more selfless attitude on my part? With whom will I share today?

*Practical steps that I will take today*

Today I will begin to heal what is hurting and acknowledge any hurt or pain. I will remember that healing takes time—lots of time.

*My prayer*

God, thank you for your great love to me. Help me to share your love with others.

*Now I will take some moments to rest with God.*

*My spiritual healing journal*

Date     Thoughts / Feelings / Insight Gained / Prayer

_____

_____

_____

_____

_____

# 6 Today with God's help: I will find someone to become my burden bearer

*Encouragement from experience*

I receive calls nearly every day from people in desperate need. One thing that strikes me is how people deal with loss. Some choose to recoil inside and keep others out. Others allow friends inside to help and encourage. But there is yet another way people deal with tragedy. Some choose to use their tragedy to grow and actually help someone else. Paul writes that we should bear each other's burdens (Galatians 6:2). To bear a burden means that someone else helps us along. They listen and they care. It is not possible for someone else to "bear my burden" if I don't "share my burden" with them.

Can you imagine receiving a note from God? Something like this: "Good morning, this is God! Today I will be handling all of your problems. Please remember that I do not need your help. If the devil happens to deliver a situation to you that you cannot handle, do not attempt to resolve it. Kindly put it in the SFGTD box (Something for God to Do). It will be addressed in MY TIME, not yours. Once the matter is placed into the box, do not hold onto it nor remove it. Holding on or removal will delay the resolution of your problem. If it is a situation that you think you are capable of handling, please consult me in prayer to be sure that it is the proper solution. Because I do not sleep, nor do I slumber (Psalm 121:4), there is no need for you to lose any sleep. Please rest my child. If you need to contact me, I am only a prayer away. My prayer line is open twenty-four hours of your day. I love you and will always be with you wherever you may go. (See Matthew 28:20.) As with all good things, pass my message on. Love, God."

*Encouragement from Scripture*

Carry each other's burdens, and in this way you will fulfill the law of Christ. (Galatians 6:2)

Happy are those whose help is the God of Jacob,
　　whose hope is in the LORD their God,
who made heaven and earth,
　　the sea, and all that is in them;
who keeps faith forever. (Psalm 146:5-6; NRSV)

*My response as I claim God's promises and grow stronger*

With whom might I share today? Whom might I listen to today? To whom will God lead me to today, to pray with and to help share their burden?

*Practical steps that I will take today*

Today I will ask God for strength and let God use others to help me. I will remember that healing takes time—lots of time.

*My prayer*

Lord, I thank you that you care. Help me to care for others and to show them your love.

*Now I will take some moments to rest with God.*

*My spiritual healing journal*

Date　　Thoughts / Feelings / Insight Gained / Prayer

_____

_____

_____

_____

_____

# 7 Today with God's help: I will leave the reasons up to God

*Encouragement from experience*

One summer, on July 30th, we received an email from my wife's sister. Her daughter desperately wanted to have a baby. After many months she finally got pregnant but sadly, the young couple found that something was terribly wrong. The email read, "There are so many things wrong with the baby; our daughter received word today that the baby will not live. The kidneys are a lot bigger than they should be, and they are full of cysts. Oh how they need our prayers. It's so hard seeing your kids go through this." On August 3rd we received this email: "Thanks for your prayers. It continues to be a hard time for everyone. They are planning a family graveside service and are going to ask Dad to say some words. They have a little casket picked out. We are now praying that God will take this child soon, another month is a long time to wait. The hardest part is seeing your kids go through something like this and there being nothing to do to make it better. We thank God that we do have a really strong support group at our church."

I've learned that there are many reasons that tragedy may come into our life. Sometimes it is because of the freedom we have to choose (Genesis 2:15-17) or it may be to warn us of danger (Psalm 78:34-35; Romans 3:10-18). I have learned that when loss and sorrow hits me, it reveals what is deep down in my heart (Job 42:1-17; Romans 5:3-5; 1 Peter 1:6-8). It's easy to say I trust in God; it is quite another to live that out in my daily life. Some severe losses seem to actually take me to the edge of eternity (Matthew 5:1-12; Romans 8:18-19)—then I find there is nothing else left except to totally trust God for help and strength. Sometimes the loss has been to loosen my grip on this life (Ecclesiastics 12:1-14), and sometimes it has been to give me an opportunity to trust God more (Job 1–42). Have you ever thought that great suffering could serve as a reminder that God's comfort is greater than suffering (2 Corinthians 12:9)? If

I never have any sorrow I would never fully understand God's faithfulness and what blessings really are all about. Tragedy can also help me draw close to God, family, and friends (2 Corinthians 1:3-4)—and even allow God to turn something around for my good (Genesis 50:20; Matthew 27:46).

### Encouragement from Scripture

"For my thoughts are not your thoughts, neither are your ways my ways," declares the LORD. "As the heavens are higher than the earth, so are my ways higher than your ways and my thoughts than your thoughts." (Isaiah 55:8-9)

### My response as I claim God's promises and grow stronger

Could it be that God is teaching me something new today? What might that be? When did I ever try to outguess God? What were the results?

### Practical steps that I will take today

Today I will acknowledge that God *is* there, God is my strength, and God is a help to me. I will remember that healing takes time—lots of time.

### My prayer

Remind me today, Lord, never to try to outguess you. Today my heart's desire is to fully trust in you and you alone.

*Now I will take some moments to rest with God.*

Date       Thoughts / Feelings / Insight Gained / Prayer

_____

_____

_____

_____

_____

# 8 Today with God's help: I will really trust God

*Encouragement from experience*

Trust is such an easy word to say but so difficult to put into practice. When I was with a group of children at a camp I used the swimming pool as a good example. Young children are often afraid to jump into the water. I would stand in the pool and explain that I was right there to catch them, but they had to "trust me." I'd have the children say the words, but then came the challenge: to put trust into action and jump. It is important that today you really trust God. Today I will let God remind me that God *does* lead people (Psalm 23), and God is faithful (Psalm 9:1, 2, 7-10). I will let God remind me that God is creator, including my creator (Psalm 139:1-6, 13-14, 23-24), and God is near me (Psalm 16:1, 2, 5-9, 11a). Many people know Psalm 23 (the "Good Shepherd" psalm). Sometimes we miss the phrase, "*through* the valley" (v. 4). God has promised to lead me carefully *through* the valley and not just leave us in the valley.

*Encouragement from Scripture*

> The LORD is my shepherd, I shall not be in want.
> He makes me lie down in green pastures;

he leads me beside still waters;
    he restores my soul.
He leads me in right paths
    for his name's sake.

Even though I walk through the darkest valley
    I fear no evil,
for you are with me;
    your rod and your staff—
    they comfort me.

You prepare a table before me
    in the presence of my enemies;
you anoint my head with oil;
    my cup overflows.

Surely goodness and mercy shall follow me
    all the days of my life,
and I will dwell in the house of the LORD
    my whole life long. (Psalm 23; NRSV)

*My response as I claim God's promises and grow stronger*

What is the valley I am being guided *through* today and what does God want to teach me?

*Practical steps that I will take today*

Today I will persist in hope knowing that God is leading me in my life. I will remember: healing takes time—lots of time.

*My prayer*

Remind me, LORD, that I am not lost *in* the valley, but that you are leading me *through* the valley.

*Now I will take some moments to rest with God.*

Date     Thoughts / Feelings / Insight Gained / Prayer

_____

_____

_____

_____

_____

## 9 Today with God's help: Because God loves me, I will let God teach me to not lose heart

*Encouragement from experience*

My wife and I were serving in our second congregation. We had a son (two years old), and my wife was expecting our second child. As sometimes is the case, something went wrong, and the doctor told her that she probably would not have the baby full term. The night of the miscarriage was traumatic for both of us. She began bleeding and the bleeding just would not stop. I called our family doctor (who was a member of our congregation, but a former military doctor who had little compassion for young couples wanting sympathy). He told me to let nature run its course. My wife continued to bleed in the night, and I called him back saying I just didn't know what to do so I was taking her to the emergency room. Before I could get her to the emergency room, she had the miscarriage at home and we both were devastated beyond words. We don't always understand why things happen as they do. In fact, things often happen to us that seem unexplainable. Though God may not offer an explanation, God will not abandon us. The writer of the Letter to the Hebrews reminds us to not lose heart (12:5).

*Encouragement from Scripture*

Endure hardship as discipline; God is treating you as sons [and daughters]. (Hebrews 12:7)

God, who comforts the downcast, comforted us. (1 Corinthians 7:6)

*My response as I claim God's promises and grow stronger*

What hardship am I feeling or experiencing today? What is God trying to show to me or teach me through this experience?

*Practical steps that I will take today*

Today I will accept life and the events of this day as they come to me. Today I will accept what comes into my life as ultimately under God's control and ability to heal. I will remember that healing takes time—lots of time.

*My prayer*

God, so often I become impatient. Forgive my impatience and give me the grace and peace to accept what you allow to come into my life.

*Now I will take some moments to rest with God.*

*My spiritual healing journal*

Date    Thoughts / Feelings / Insight Gained / Prayer

_____

_____

_____

_____

_____

# 10 Today with God's help: I will remember that when things are down I will look up

*Encouragement from experience*

It was Christmas Eve when the telephone rang at our home. The call was from parents of a junior high boy who had accidentally shot himself in the right eye with a BB gun. Their son was in emergency surgery that night, and they needed emotional and spiritual help. I arrived at the hospital to encourage the parents. After hours of waiting the doctor came out with the news—the boy would lose his eye. At a time like that, there is no place to turn except to Scripture and to God. In Psalm 73 I find some steps to help me to *both* "cry out" *and* "be quiet" and to realize that I simply do not understand. This psalm helps me to look into the presence of God, to look at the big picture, and not to lose perspective. It helps me to reevaluate my thinking and to realize that God still loves us.

*Encouragement from Scripture*

> Nevertheless I am continually with you;
>     you hold me by my right hand.
> You guide me with your counsel,
>     and afterward you will receive me with honor.
>         (Psalm 73:23-24; NRSV)

*My response as I claim God's promises and grow stronger*

Have I had a "sanctuary" experience where I was truly in the presence of God? Where and when? What happened? What am I doing to keep that faith perspective alive? How can I cultivate my faith, my relationship with God?

Today I will make a choice to not be myopic. I will choose to look beyond today and to remember God's precious promises. I will remember that God sees the bigger picture and I will remember that healing takes time—lots of time.

*My prayer*

My desire is to love and serve you, God. When things are down, help me to look up to *you!*

*Now I will take some moments to rest with God.*

*My spiritual healing journal*

Date        Thoughts / Feelings / Insight Gained / Prayer

_____

_____

_____

_____

_____


# **I I Today with God's help: I will accept God as my God of comfort in grief**

*Encouragement from experience*

Those who have worked through the grief process tell us that a grieving person goes through five stages. The first is shock and denial followed by a tendency to resentment and anger, which leads to acceptance, and finally readjustment.[2] Each of these

[2] Ibid. See above, p. 10.

stages takes time. Isaiah 43 gives comfort. Today I will accept God as my God of comfort in grief. Some ways to find comfort in grief are to remember that God is always with us, comforts us, and lets my grieving open a door of opportunity to help someone else. It is also important to focus on God and God's love.

### Encouragement from Scripture

Fear not, for I have redeemed you; I have summoned you by name; you are mine. When you pass through the waters, I will be with you; and when you pass through the rivers, they will not sweep over you. When you walk through the fire, you will not be burned; the flames will not set you ablaze. For I am the LORD, your God, the Holy One of Israel, your Savior. Since you are precious and honored in my sight, and because I love you, I will give men in exchange for you, and people in exchange for your life. Do not be afraid, for I am with you. (Isaiah 43:1-7)

### My response as I claim God's promises and grow stronger

What is God saying to me today about getting on with my life?

### Practical steps that I will take today

Today I will remember that loss and grief resurrect old issues, feelings, and unresolved conflicts from my past. I will accept the fact that God truly loves and cares for me. I will remember that healing takes time—lots of time.

### My prayer

Thank you for your comforting hand during times of sorrow, loss, and grief.

### Now I will take some moments to rest with God.

Date    Thoughts / Feelings / Insight Gained / Prayer

_____

_____

_____

_____

_____

# 12 Today with God's help: I will acknowledge that when God makes a promise, God keeps it

*Encouragement from experience*

Promises are pretty amazing when you think about it. A promise is as good as the person who makes the promise. When we were preparing to leave Ohio to move to Arizona, we put an ad in the local newspaper to sell our dining room set. The community was a small rural area where everyone knew each other. A man telephoned us asking about the dining room set that we had advertised. After we told him about it, he wanted to come and look at it. When he arrived, he was in an old pick up truck, and he was wearing a dirty work shirt and jeans. After a few minutes, he said, "I'll take it." We said great and were getting ready to discuss payment and get a receipt when he suddenly pulled six crumpled up one hundred dollar bills from his pocket. He laid them on the dining room table and said, you have my word—do I have yours? We said of course and he told us he would be back in a week or two to pick it up! He promised us, and we promised him—and that was enough. Scripture, God's Word, is filled with promises. Accepting God's promises is a key to healing and peace in life. The writer of Hebrews gives some principles about God's promises. Hebrews 6 includes three principles about God's promises: When God makes a promise, the promise is certain (vv. 13, 14, 17). When God makes a promise, the promise is on God's timeline not ours (v. 15). When God makes a promise, I must rest on that promise and be encouraged (v. 18).

### Encouragement from Scripture

When God made his promise to Abraham, since there was no one greater for him to swear by, he swore by himself, saying, "I will surely bless you and give you many descendants." And so after waiting patiently, Abraham received what was promised. (Hebrews 6:13-15)

### My response as I claim God's promises and grow stronger

When was I frustrated with waiting for God to do something in my life? How can I specifically claim the certainty of God's promises in my life? What can I do or say that will show I am claiming God's promises?

### Practical steps that I will take today

Today I will remember that I am not alone. I will remember that others care and that God cares. I will remember that healing takes time—lots of time.

### My prayer

I know, God, that when you make a promise, you keep it. I thank you for your faithfulness to me every day.

*Now I will take some moments to rest with God.*

Date     Thoughts / Feelings / Insight Gained / Prayer

_____

_____

_____

_____

_____

## 13 Today with God's help: I will let God teach me to "fear not"

*Encouragement from experience*

When was a time when you were really afraid? Was it in the midst of a terrible storm or hurricane? Or was it, perhaps, a massive earthquake or raging fire? I remember a time when my wife and I were having dinner in a lovely restaurant on the seventeenth floor of a hotel on the West Coast. We were overlooking the ocean. All of a sudden the lights went out, and everyone in the restaurant became very quiet. Somehow we all knew that something was wrong—very wrong—and you could feel slight panic creep in. It may have been because it was in an area where major earthquakes happen frequently—or it just may have been instinctive—but people knew this was not just a normal power failure. Sure enough, someone came around telling people to move to the exits and to begin walking down the many flights of stairs. There is something about a crowd that feeds fear, and it seemed that with every floor people moved faster and faster and began pushing one another.

Psalms 34 and 40 tell of David's fears but also of God's faithfulness. These two psalms give some steps toward deliverance from fear: I must acknowledge my weakness and I must lay hold of God's power and gain strength.

*Encouragement from Scripture*

I sought the LORD, and he answered me,
   and delivered me from all my fears.

. . . . . . . . . . . . . . . . . . . . . .

O taste and see that the LORD is good;
   Happy are those who take refuge in him.

. . . . . . . . . . . . . . . . . . . . . .

The eyes of the LORD are on the righteous,
   and his ears are open to their cry.
The face of the LORD is against evildoers,
   to cut off the remembrance memory of them from the earth.
When the righteous cry for help, the LORD hears,
   and rescues them from all their troubles.
The LORD is near to the brokenhearted,
   and saves those who are crushed in spirit.
      (Psalm 34:4, 8, 15-18; NRSV)

*My response as I claim God's promises and grow stronger*

In what way is Psalm 34 also my own testimony? (See verse 22; also Romans 8:1).

Which helps me most with present troubles: Remembering God's actions in the past or claiming God's promises for the future? (See Psalm 40.)

*Practical steps that I will take today*

Today I will be thankful for this day as a gift from God. I will remember that healing takes time—lots of time.

*My prayer*

God, remove all fear from within me, help me to trust in you. Help me to feel safe.

*Now I will take some moments to rest with God.*

Date     Thoughts / Feelings / Insight Gained / Prayer

_____

_____

_____

_____

_____

## 14 Today with God's help: I will move from trials to triumph

*Encouragement from experience*

Our two children took piano lessons from a good friend who was an encourager. This lady knew how to move a student from trials to triumph. Some of her favorite phrases were, "I know you can do it," "That was great," and "You've got it!" In James 1:1-4, 12 the writer gives some lessons God has for us concerning life's challenges. These verses will help you move from trials to triumph today. As you read these verses, you will see that there is an attitude you must have about your problems (v. 1). There is a purpose you must discover (vv. 3-4). And there are ultimate results you will experience (vv. 4, 12). To move me from trials to triumph say: God has allowed things to come into our lives, and we are under God's care. God is in control. God is faithful, and God will keep us safe as we continue our journeys. God will bring you out of this in God's time—and God will make the trial a blessing.

*Encouragement from Scripture*

You do not have, because you do not ask God. (James 4:1-4, 12)

*My response as I claim God's promises and grow stronger*

How is God helping me through trials I am facing today? What do I need to specifically ask God for today, to give me victory?

*Practical steps that I will take today*

Today I will be confident that God is in charge of every step of my life. I will remember that healing takes time—lots of time.

*My prayer*

Forgive my lack of faith. For your glory, give me your strength for this day

*Now I will take some moments to rest with God.*

*My spiritual healing journal*

Date        Thoughts / Feelings / Insight Gained / Prayer

_____

_____

_____

_____

_____


# 15 Today with God's help: I will grasp lessons about a positive attitude

*Encouragement from experience*

Once when I was with a patient before surgery, I intended to read some Scripture and offer a word of encouragement and prayer for God's guidance and peace. After I read and said a few words of encouragement, I was just about to pray when a nurse came to the man's bed. She checked his chart, made sure that everything was in order, and told me that he would be going to surgery very shortly. The doctor and the nurse had said earlier that attitude was extremely important prior to surgery. I remember the man saying over and over to me and to his wife that he was sure that he would not come out of surgery alive. I also remember that nurse who came in. She leaned over the bed and looked right into his eyes and she said very sternly, "No more of that negative talk now. I've been a nurse for over fifteen years and know that the attitude going into surgery greatly impacts the results and the recovery." Attitude! Today, whatever the situation—grasp that positive attitude.

Whatever your situation is today, why not say "I will choose to have a positive attitude"?

### Encouragement from Scripture

I know what it is to be in need, and I know what it is to have plenty. I have learned the secret of being content in any and every situation, whether well fed or hungry, whether living in plenty or in want. I can do everything through him who gives me strength. (Philippians 4:12-13)

### My response as I claim God's promises and grow stronger

Concerning a trial I have experienced, what pressures did it bring on my faith? What wisdom did I gain through it? On a scale of 1 to 10 what is my "perseverance level"? How well have I stood the test?

### Practical steps that I will take today

Today, I will seek to discover God's purpose for my life. I will experience God's joy. I will keep my focus on healing and keep my sense of humor, no matter what. I will remember that healing takes time—lots of time.

*My prayer*

This day, Lord, I do want to have a positive attitude with your strength. Help me to live my life for you today. Fill me with your loving spirit.

*Now I will take some moments to rest with God.*

*My spiritual healing journal*

Date       Thoughts / Feelings / Insight Gained / Prayer

---

---

---

---

---

## 16 Today with God's help: I will say "God is a God of miracles"

*Encouragement from experience*

God is a God of miracles—really. Sure, we look around and see some terrible things happening, but don't miss out on the miracles happening every day. Each day, after I have completed my hospital visits, I walk over to the nursery and take a few minutes to look at some miracles. Oh, sometimes I see a baby who needs treatment, but God is there. Sometimes God, in mystery, allows a tiny child to die. But God always gives the strength to carry on.

How about the miracle of the sunset and sunrise? Watch during a thunder storm and notice the magnificent display of God's power in the lightning. Or perhaps just stop for a moment and watch the tiny ants as they rush about, or the birds nesting or eagles soaring. God is a God of miracles; we just sometimes miss the miracles around us.

There are at least three things about the miracle in Mark 5:35-43. There was a desperate request (vv. 22-24). There was a devastating report (vv. 35, 36). There were dynamic and delightful results (vv. 37-43).

### Encouragement from Scripture

While Jesus was still speaking, some men came from the house of Jairus, the synagogue ruler. "Your daughter is dead," they said. "Why bother the teacher any more?" Ignoring what they said, Jesus told the synagogue ruler, "Don't be afraid; just believe." He took her by the hand and said to her, "Little girl, I say to you, get up!" Immediately the girl stood up and walked around (she was twelve years old). At this they were completely astonished. He gave strict orders not to let anyone know about this, and told them to give her something to eat. (Mark 5:35-43)

### My response as I claim God's promises and grow stronger

How have I been like the men in this story, thinking there is no hope? Or like the mourners in the passage? Have I ever laughed at the things or ways of God? When did I last hear Jesus say the words, "Don't be afraid, just believe"?

### Practical steps that I will take today

Today I will grow from my experiences. I will remember that healing takes time—lots of time.

### My prayer

God, let me hear your words today, "Don't be afraid, just believe." I do want to believe in you and your grace alone. Give me the strength to obey you today.

*Now I will take some moments to rest with God.*

*My spiritual healing journal*

Date      Thoughts / Feelings / Insight Gained / Prayer

_____

_____

_____

_____

_____

# 17 Today with God's help: I will let God teach me about the storm of caregiving

*Encouragement from experience*

I was sitting in the living room watching a bird guard the little birdfeeder we had hanging on the patio. I realized that one bird, who was guarding the feeder selfishly, wanting it all, actually became a prisoner by guarding the feeder. The bird lost its freedom. Sometimes as caregivers we feel that we have lost our freedom. We are caught in one spot, not guarding but caring for another. It is so easy to lose perspective and become myopic in the little things. Jesus said that he cares for everything, even the smallest detail in our lives. If you feel trapped, let go and let God fill your life with freedom. Allow those who care and want to help you, help you.

*Encouragement from Scripture*

Call on me in the day of trouble;
  I will deliver you, and you shall glorify me.
    (Psalm 50:15; NRSV)

*My response as I claim God's promises and grow stronger*

How has God been my refuge in recent days? What am I facing today that will call for God's extra help in being my refuge?

*Practical steps that I will take today*

Today I will remember that God knows my limitations, and I will let God energize me. I will remember that healing takes time—lots of time.

*My prayer*

As I face the storms of life, give me eyes to see that you are still guiding me every day through every storm.

*Now I will take some moments to rest with God.*

*My spiritual healing journal*

Date        Thoughts / Feelings / Insight Gained / Prayer

_____

_____

_____

_____

_____

# 18 Today with God's help: I will not worry

*Encouragement from experience*

Jesus used the example of birds to remind us not to worry. We have a large tree in our front yard and the birds love to build nests in that tree. It is fascinating to see how they work flying here and there to bring bits and pieces to build their nest. In Matthew 6:25-34 Jesus gives several reasons why we should not worry: Worry is really being unfaithful to God (v. 25). Worry causes us to think that God does not care (vv. 26-30). Worry weakens our faith (vv. 31-33). Worry diminishes our future (v. 34).

*Encouragement from Scripture*

Therefore I tell you, do not worry about your life, what you will eat or drink; or about your body, what you will wear. Is not life more important than food, and the body more important than clothes? Look at the birds of the air; they do not sow or reap or store away in barns, and yet your heavenly Father feeds them. Are you not much more valuable than they? Who of you by worrying can add a single hour to his life? And why do you worry about clothes? See how the lilies of the field grow. They do not labor or spin. (Matthew 6:25-34)

*My response as I claim God's promises and grow stronger*

In what ways have I seen God provide for my basic needs?

*Practical steps that I will take today*

Today I will acknowledge the power of a good friend and accept the power of God's Word. I will spend some time alone reading the Bible for spiritual strength. I will cherish the personal relationships that I do have. I will remember that healing takes time—lots of time.

*My prayer*

Help me not to worry today, Loving God. Remind me of your abiding presence in my life.

*Now I will take some moments to rest with God.*

*My spiritual healing journal*

Date       Thoughts / Feelings / Insight Gained / Prayer

_____

_____

_____

_____

_____

# 19 Today with God's help: I will let God remove all my fear and worry

*Encouragement from experience*

One morning when I was at the hospital to make some visits, I stepped into the elevator with another visitor. Just before the door closed, along came a man in a uniform pushing a large machine into the elevator. The three of us were quietly standing there as we pushed our buttons for various floors. The door closed. The woman broke the silence with these words, "Wow, I'm sure glad you won't be using that big machine on me—it looks pretty scary with all those tubes and gadgets." The man in the uniform replied, "No need to worry about that—this is a floor cleaning machine!"

In Matthew 6:25-34 Jesus gives some reasons why worry is wrong. The apostle Paul gives encouragement on how to overcome worry: He said that he learned to be content, no matter what his circumstances. Paul wrote in Philippians 4 and in 1 Timothy 6 that nothing is gained when we worry, except to make things worse.

### Encouragement from Scripture

I am not saying this because I am in need, for I have learned to be content whatever the circumstances. I know what it is to be in need, and I know what it is to have plenty. I have learned the secret of being content in any and every situation, whether well fed or hungry, whether living in plenty or in want. (Philippians 4:11-12)

But godliness with contentment is great gain. For we brought nothing into the world, and we can take nothing out of it. But if we have food and clothing, we will be content with that. (1 Timothy 6:6-8)

### My response as I claim God's promises and grow stronger

How content am I at this very moment? Why or why not? What needs to happen in my life to help me let go and just let God take care of things?

### Practical steps that I will take today

Today I will be aware that worry and fear are life's great distracters. Today, with God's help I will let God remove all fear and worry from my day. I will remember that healing takes time—lots of time.

### My prayer

God, I know that there is no need for me to worry, because you are in charge of my life. Remove all fear and worry from my life today.

### Now I will take some moments to rest with God.

Date     Thoughts / Feelings / Insight Gained / Prayer

_____

_____

_____

_____

_____

## 20 Today with God's help: I will rejoice in the fact that there's no disappointment in Jesus

*Encouragement from experience*

Once while I was at a camp in the mountains in northern California, I saw a little sign that read, "Follow this trail to the little brown church on the hill." Intrigued, I began hiking up the mountain. I hiked and hiked following the turns and inclines until coming to another sign encouraging me to keep going because that little brown church was just around the next bend. This went on for a couple of hours until the sign read, "You are there, just two hundred feet to the little brown church." When I reached the top of the mountain, there it was, a little brown church, about five inches tall! In some ways I was disappointed—but I had to grin. My expectations were far different from reality. Isn't that true in life, especially when it comes to loss and sorrow? We expect God to make everything right—instantly—but it just does not happen. God knows the timing; our job is to trust in God's guidance and strength. Scripture gives biblical principles to remind us that there is no disappointment in Jesus. We must realize that God is in control of all circumstances. We must recognize people for what they are—*human*. We must remember our goal in life—to walk in the same manner as Jesus walked. (See 1 John 2:6.)

*Encouragement from Scripture*

May our Lord Jesus Christ himself and God our Father, who loved us and by his grace gave us eternal encouragement and good hope, encourage your hearts and strengthen you in every good deed and word. (2 Thessalonians 2:16-17)

*My response as I claim God's promises and grow stronger*

When was the last time I felt disappointment? Why? How would remembering that God is in control help heal that disappointment?

*Practical steps that I will take today*

Today I will leave the impossible part up to God, I will make needed adjustments, and I will make amends for past failures and then let go and move on. I will remember that healing takes time—lots of time.

*My prayer*

God, I know that life does have its disappointments, but remind me that there are no disappointments in you.

*Now I will take some moments to rest with God.*

*My spiritual healing journal*

Date        Thoughts / Feelings / Insight Gained / Prayer

_____

_____

_____

_____

_____

# 21 | Today with God's help: I will let God win my battles in life

*Encouragement from experience*

You may have seen the movie, *What about Bob?* that was released some years ago. It was a very funny movie about a psychiatrist and his patient whose name was Bob. The psychiatrist kept telling Bob, the patient, that he had to take it one day at a time, that taking "baby steps" was the key.

If you want to win the battles in life, you take it one day at a time, "baby steps." God will win the victory but it will be in God's way and at God's time. Joshua 5 and 6 remind us that God wins the battles of life. Rather than our fighting in our own strength, we must let God win. For the Israelites, as God won their battle, some important things happened. They restored the sacred symbolic institutions of circumcision and the Passover (5:1-12). They had an encounter with God (5:13-6:5). The Israelites obeyed God—and let God win the battle (6:6-27).

*Encouragement from Scripture*

For God did not give us a spirit of timidity, but a spirit of power, of love and of self-discipline. (2 Timothy 1:7)

Even if I should choose to boast, I would not be a fool, because I would be speaking the truth. But I refrain, so no one will think more of me than is warranted by what I do or say. (2 Corinthians 12:6)

*My response as I claim God's promises and grow stronger*

What specific battles are going on in my life today? What is my response to God?

*Practical steps that I will take today*

Today I will become aware of resources available to help me. (Those at the end of this book may help.) I will utilize both human and divine resources. I will remember that healing takes time—lots of time.

*My prayer*

O God, for too long I have been trying to fight life's battles, today I release that fighting and let you take over.

*Now I will take some moments to rest with God.*

*My spiritual healing journal*

Date      Thoughts / Feelings / Insight Gained / Prayer

_____

_____

_____

_____

_____

# 22 Today with God's help: I will say, "Don't be afraid; just believe"

*Encouragement from experience*

A little girl who was dying of leukemia asked the nurse for a crying doll. When the nurse asked why, she replied, "Mommy and I need to cry. Mommy won't cry in front of me, and I can't cry if Mommy doesn't. If we had a crying doll, all three of us could cry together. I think we'd feel better."

There are times that a good cry really helps. But then comes the gentle reminder—don't be afraid—just believe. In Mark 5:35-43, Jesus said something to a synagogue ruler that was amazing and a strong reminder for us today. Jesus said those very words, "Don't be afraid, just believe." Sure, you may need a good cry—but be sure not to miss the words of Jesus when he tells you not to be afraid, just believe.

### Encouragement from Scripture

Ignoring what they said, Jesus told the synagogue ruler, "Don't be afraid; just believe." (Mark 5:36)

### My response as I claim God's promises and grow stronger

What is the relationship between crisis and faith in my life? How have I been like the those who thought there was no hope? (Mark 5:35). Or like the mourners? (Mark 5:40). I wonder how the synagogue ruler felt when he heard the words of Jesus? (Mark 5:36) When did I last hear Jesus say to me the words, "Don't be afraid, just believe"?

### Practical steps that I will take today

Today I will set some goals for myself, and with God's help those goals will be reached. Today, I will search for meaning from my adversity, acknowledging that Jesus said not to be afraid, but to just believe. I will remember that healing takes time—lots of time.

### My prayer

Grant me the strength this day to not only hear your words of encouragement, but to obey you, God. As you spoke through your Son Jesus to the ruler of the synagogue, I claim those words for my life.

*Now I will take some moments to rest with God.*

Date      Thoughts / Feelings / Insight Gained / Prayer

_____

_____

_____

_____

_____

# 23 Today with God's help: I will take courage and not be afraid

*Encouragement from experience*

It is interesting how fear affects us. We sometimes blow things out of proportion. The doctor may order a test or procedure, and, while waiting for the results, we let fear of the unknown build up. I joke about going to the doctor's office for a simple checkup and beginning to get anxious when the doctor turns around and begins opening drawers and pulling things out! I joke about seeing him whip around with this huge needle, and I yell—stop!

We fear the unknown and find it hard to let God take over in matters of life. Mark 6:7-56 records three ways God meets needs. I can apply these to my own life today as God meets my needs: When I'm hungry God provides (vv. 35-42). When I'm helpless God gives the divine presence (vv. 45-52). When I'm hurting God gives divine power (vv. 53-56).

*Encouragement from Scripture*

Keep your lives free from the love of money and be content with what you have, because God has said, "Never will I leave you; never will I forsake you." (Hebrews 13:5)

`. . .` teaching them to obey everything I have commanded you. And surely I am with you always, to the very end of the age. (Matthew 28:20)

*My response as I claim God's promises and grow stronger*

How did Jesus' words in the Gospel of Mark (6:50) speak to that storm? In what specific areas of my life do I need to take courage and not be afraid?

*Practical steps that I will take today*

Today I will make a conscious effort to walk through this day without fear. I will remember that healing takes time—lots of time.

*My prayer*

God, remind me that you are always with me. Just as you cared for the disciples, you truly care for me. Help me not to be afraid.

*Now I will take some moments to rest with God.*

*My spiritual healing journal*

Date      Thoughts / Feelings / Insight Gained / Prayer

_____

_____

_____

_____

_____

# 24 Today with God's help: I will experience God's wonderful peace

*Encouragement from experience*

Someone said, "What you eat doesn't give you ulcers, it's what's eating you." We're all looking for peace. Our society has become an escape society. We're off to ballgames and entertainment. We need to get away from it all. We want to get away from the summer heat, we want to get away on vacation with the hope that we will return refreshed and filled with peace. But many persons today are looking for God's peace in the wrong places. Hebrews 13:17-25 gives us a picture of God's wonderful peace. God's wonderful peace gives us provision (v. 20) and God's wonderful peace gives us God's purpose (v. 21).

*Encouragement from Scripture*

"Peace I leave with you; my peace I give you. I do not give to you as the world gives. Do not let your hearts be troubled and do not be afraid." (John 14:27)

"I have told you these things, so that in me you may have peace. In this world you will have trouble. But take heart! I have overcome world." (John 16:33)

*Practical steps that I will take today*

Today I will be myself. I will relax and enjoy God's wonderful peace. Today I will adjust to new realities and I will remember that healing takes time—lots of time.

*My prayer*

Give me a new, fresh sense of your peace today. I trust in you and you alone.

*Now I will take some moments to rest with God.*

Date     Thoughts / Feelings / Insight Gained / Prayer

_____

_____

_____

_____

_____

# 25 Today with God's help: I will accept the fact there is help for hurting hearts

*Encouragement from experience*

Someone from another church visited our morning worship service. I became aware of the fact that this man had recently lost his wife. I hesitated to make a home visit so instead I decided to contact the senior pastor of his church. After a week went by, I wondered if his pastor had made a call on the man; I also wondered if the man would be back in our worship service. You guessed it: the next week he was back with us. At this point, I felt compelled to talk with the man's pastor, my colleague. When I met the pastor for breakfast I shared with him that one of his members was in our worship service several Sundays. I was shocked at his response. To my amazement, the pastor used a phrase that haunted me, he said: "that crybaby." Indeed the man was extremely emotional, but for good reason. The man was in desperate need of love, care, and sympathy. He needed help in the grieving process.

In many cases, we misunderstand the healing process in thinking that people should "get over it." Healing takes time and sometimes that means years. One thing to remember is that there is hope and help. There is help for your hurting heart. When hurt or pain comes into our life, there is a tendency to pull back. The very thing we need to do is what we do not do. We need God and we need other people for strength and encouragement. The psalmist wrote about that. Try reading Psalm 91 to gain strength for a hurting heart.

*Encouragement from Scripture*

> You who live in the shelter of the Most High,
>   who abide in the shadow of the Almighty,
> will say to the LORD, "My refuge and my fortress;
>   my God, in whom I trust." (Psalm 91:1-2; NRSV)

*My response as I claim God's promises and grow stronger*

What does it mean to make God my refuge? As I think about any potential harm that could come in my life, do I truly believe that angels will be helping me? (See Psalm 91:11.)

*Practical steps that I will take today*

Today I will ask for God's guidance, and I will seek help from friends. I will remember that healing takes time—lots of time.

*My prayer*

As I live this day, O God, by your strength, help me to rest in your shadow. Remind me today that you are my refuge and my fortress.

*Now I will take some moments to rest with God.*

*My spiritual healing journal*

Date      Thoughts / Feelings / Insight Gained / Prayer

_____

_____

_____

# 26 Today with God's help: I will claim God's promises during my times of loneliness

*Encouragement from experience*

A friend of mine owns a sailboat, and he and I used to sail from Marina Del Ray to Catalina Island together. One day he told me to take over the controls, assuring me that the instruments would do their job; all I had to do was keep watch on the instruments and stay focused on our goal ahead. I learned a great lesson about trust as I let the instruments guide us—all the time remembering how wonderful it is to know that our sovereign God knows what is ahead in our life.

My job is to trust in God's promises. In the New Testament we read about Bartimaeus who was blind. Jesus performed a miracle, and Bartimaeus received his sight. We see in this story God's faithfulness. Jesus was faithful to the blind man when he saw the blind man's condition and heard the man's cry. God provided the cure for the man. God is faithful to us today. Our job is to claim God's promises, even during our times of loneliness.

*Encouragement from Scripture*

Then they came to Jericho. As Jesus and his disciples, together with a large crowd, were leaving the city, a blind man, Bartimaeus (that is, the Son of Timaeus), was sitting by the roadside begging. When he heard that it was Jesus of Nazareth, he began to shout, "Jesus, Son of David, have mercy on me!" Many rebuked him and told him to be quiet, but he shouted all the more, "Son of David, have mercy on me!" Jesus stopped and said, "Call him." So they called to the blind man, "Cheer up! On your feet! He's calling you." Throwing his cloak aside, he jumped to his feet and came to Jesus. "What do you want me to do for you?" Jesus asked him. The blind man said, "Rabbi, I want to see." "Go," said Jesus, "your faith has healed you." Immediately he received his sight and followed Jesus along the road. (Mark 10:46-52)

*My response as I claim God's promises and grow stronger*

If Jesus asked me, "What do you want me to do for you?" what would I say?

*Practical steps that I will take today*

How has God been faithful to me this week? I will think of at least one way. Today I will remember that healing takes time— lots of time.

*My prayer*

God, thank *you* for your faithfulness. Help me to love and serve you.

*Now I will take some moments to rest with God.*

*My spiritual healing journal*

Date     Thoughts / Feelings / Insight Gained / Prayer

_____

_____

_____

_____

_____

# 27 Today with God's help: I will claim God's cleansing from guilt

*Encouragement from experience*

Guilt can be crippling. But God's love can free us from guilt because Jesus has paid the penalty for all of our sins. Someone in our congregation once told me that he had heard of a friend who felt guilty about cheating on his income tax. He said that he actually returned $150, cash, in an envelope to the IRS. He included a note saying that he felt guilty for cheating on his return . . . and that he would send the rest if he still felt guilty!

God brings things to our minds and hearts, and prompts us to follow the divine lead. Perhaps you feel guilty or stressed out today. This is your opportunity to make things right with God and claim God's forgiveness. We must place our trust in God and ask for forgiveness. The Scriptures presents several facts about being cleansed from guilt: I will accept the fact that complete forgiveness *is* possible (Hebrews 10:1-3); I will move on with my life when God or someone else forgives me (Hebrews 10:17, 18, 22; 13:18). I will accept myself as God does.

*Encouragement from Scripture*

For God so loved the world that he gave his one and only Son, that whoever believes in him shall not perish but have eternal life. For God did not send his Son into the world to condemn the world, but to save the world through him. Whoever believes in him is not condemned, but whoever does not believe stands condemned already because he has not believed in the name of God's one and only Son. (John 3:16-18)

*My response as I claim God's promises and grow stronger*

What am I feeling guilty about today, and why? As I consider the steps of cleansing and forgiveness, which steps do I need to claim? If I know of someone who is hurting, why not call and encourage that person?

*Practical steps that I will take today*

Today I will accept God's forgiveness, and I will claim God's cleansing for my life. Today I claim God's grace for my life; I will remember that healing takes time—lots of time.

*My prayer*

Right now, Lord, I claim your cleansing for my life. Empower me today.

*Now I will take some moments to rest with God.*

*My spiritual healing journal*

Date      Thoughts / Feelings / Insight Gained / Prayer

_____

_____

_____

_____

_____

# 28 Today with God's help: I will break any bonds of bitterness

*Encouragement from experience*

A psychologist friend of mine once told me that bitterness is like a built-in trash compactor, except that the trash compactor is broken and begins eating itself! Bitterness is like that; it eats us up inside. To break the bonds of bitterness, I need to recognize bitterness for what it is—sin. I want to keep from hurting others by displaying kindness. I want to practice forgiveness according to God's divine standard. I want to ask God to help me break the bonds of bitterness.

### Encouragement from Scripture

Finally, brothers [and sisters], whatever is true, whatever is noble, whatever is right, whatever is pure, whatever is lovely, whatever is admirable—if anything is excellent or praiseworthy—think about such things. Whatever you have learned or received or heard from me, or seen in me—put it into practice. And the God of peace will be with you. (Philippians 4:8-9)

Do not repay evil with evil or insult with insult, but with blessing, because to this you were called so that you may inherit a blessing. (1 Peter 3:9)

Be kind and compassionate to one another, forgiving each other, just as in Christ God forgave you. (Ephesians 4:32)

### My response as I claim God's promises and grow stronger

What is it that is eating away at me today? How is that affecting me?

### Practical steps that I will take today

Today I will respect differences in people and with God's help will let go of bitterness and anger. I will remember that healing takes time—lots of time.

### My prayer

Forgive me my bitterness. Grant me freedom today!

### Now I will take some moments to rest with God.

Date     Thoughts / Feelings / Insight Gained / Prayer

_____

_____

_____

_____

_____

# 29 Today with God's help: I will learn about coping with anxiety

### Encouragement from experience

The washing machine was broken, the phone was ringing, and she had a terrible headache. She just couldn't face another hour of the baby crying, and she had just reached the breaking point. As she lifted the one-year-old into highchair and leaned over to put her head on the tray to begin to cry, the one-year-old—without a word—took his pacifier out of his mouth and pushed it into hers!

The New Testament word for being anxious is *merimnao*. It means, "to divide," that is, to be mentally torn apart. Here are some simple biblical steps to help you cope with anxiety: Begin trusting and stop worrying; begin "turning lose." Stop straining too much, and begin a regular time alone with God and get into God's Word. Select a specific time and place where you will spend at least fifteen minutes in reading the Scriptures and praying daily.

### Encouragement from Scripture

Do not be anxious about anything, but in everything, by prayer and petition, with thanksgiving, present your requests to

God. And the peace of God, which transcends all understanding, will guard your hearts and your minds in Christ Jesus. (Philippians 4:6-7)

*My response as I claim God's promises and grow stronger*

What am I anxious about at this moment? Will worrying about it make it any better?

*Practical steps that I will take today*

Today I will not dwell on any regrets. Instead I will thank God for the blessings in my life. Today I will not withdraw from involving myself with others. Instead I will make a conscious decision to get together with friends. I will remember that healing takes time—lots of time.

*My prayer*

God, today I want to live this day free from anxiety. With your help, I will claim your promises, accept your blessings, and let you fill my day with joy.

*Now I will take some moments to rest with God.*

*My spiritual healing journal*

Date       Thoughts / Feelings / Insight Gained / Prayer

_____

_____

_____

_____

_____

# 30 Today with God's help: I will let God guide me through my losses

*Encouragement from experience*

Excitement filled the house as our son packed his things and was off to university. It was an exciting time but my feelings caught me off guard one night. My wife was asleep and I couldn't stop thinking and wondering about how quickly the years had slipped away. I got out of bed and quietly walked down the hallway to our son's room. I quietly walked into that empty room and sat on the floor gazing at an old soccer ball, an old baseball bat and glove, some large posters on the wall, and various personal items he had left while away at school.

Losses in life are so varied. The loss of loved ones through death is traumatic but divorce or children leaving are deep and often painful experiences for parents. At times, such as the night in our son's room years ago, I need to be reminded to let God guide me through my loss.

We read in Mark 5:21-34 about a woman Jesus healed. Read the story; notice that in her condition she was diseased, desperate, and destitute (vv. 25-26). Notice her cure, as Jesus came by and touched her and gave her healing (vv. 27-29). Notice her confession. When something good happens to us we want to tell others (vv. 30-34).

*Encouragement from Scripture*

And a woman was there who had been subject to bleeding for twelve years. She had suffered a great deal under the care of many doctors and had spent all she had; yet instead of getting better she grew worse. When she heard about Jesus, she came up behind him in the crowd and touched his cloak, because she thought, "If I just touch his clothes, I will be healed." Immediately her bleeding stopped and she felt in her body that she was freed from her suffering. At once Jesus realized that power had gone out from him. He turned around in the crowd and asked, "Who touched my clothes?" "You see the people crowding against you," his disciples answered, "and yet you can ask, 'Who touched me?'" But Jesus kept looking around to see who had done it. Then the woman, knowing what had happened to her, came and fell at his feet and, trembling with fear, told him the whole truth. He said to her, "Daughter, your faith has healed you. Go in peace and be freed from your suffering." (Mark 5:25-43)

*My response as I claim God's promises and grow stronger*

How do I feel when others minimize my grief? What might I do about that?

*Practical steps that I will take today*

Today I will remember that God guides me *through* my losses. I will remember that healing takes time—lots of time.

*My prayer*

Give me strength this day to conquer loss and be strong.

*Now I will take some moments to rest with God.*

*My spiritual healing journal*

Date      Thoughts / Feelings / Insight Gained / Prayer

_____

_____

_____

_____

_____

# 31 | Today with God's help: I will have victory even when life seems to be falling apart

*Encouragement from experience*

When I was in junior high school, I took a class in wood-working. Little did I know back then that God was going to teach me a great lesson about life. I was learning how to use a lathe. As I worked on the block of wood on that lathe, I became aware of the image in Scripture: God is the potter, we are the clay. (See Isaiah 29:16; Jeremiah 18:1-6.) I was learning that God is the one shaping my life. I must learn to trust in God's guidance in all situations.

Most people know about the biblical character Job. He was a godly man whose life fell apart. In reading about the tragic events of Job's life one can see three views: There was Job's view, which was frustration, yet he affirmed God's sovereignty. There were Job's friends' views that were not helpful at all. There was God's view, which gives us some insight into the bigger picture. In reading through the Book of Job we see Job's faithfulness to God even in the face of his many tragedies. When we finally let go and let God have God's way, we gain the victory.

*Encouragement from Scripture*

At this, Job got up and tore his robe and shaved his head. Then he fell to the ground in worship and said: "Naked I came from my mother's womb, and naked I will depart. The LORD gave and the LORD has taken away; may the name of the LORD be praised." (Job 1:20-21)

*My response as I claim God's promises and grow stronger*

When did it seem that my life had fallen apart, and what was my response?

Today I will thank God for life itself, and I will remember that healing takes time—lots of time.

## My prayer

Help me to be thankful for every breath that you give to me this day.

*Now I will take some moments to rest with God.*

## My spiritual healing journal

Date     Thoughts / Feelings / Insight Gained / Prayer

_____

_____

_____

_____

_____

# 32 Today with God's help: I will learn from Job about empty words and shallow answers

## Encouragement from experience

I was a young associate minister serving in a fairly large congregation, and I thought my job was secure. However, after being on staff for only two years, the senior minister resigned and I was left to hold the entire congregation together for a year as they searched for a new senior minister. When the new senior pastor was found I remember the sinking feeling in my heart when he told me that he would be bringing staff with him—which meant that I needed to find another place of service. My heart sunk into the depth of despair and the last thing I wanted to hear was clichés and Bible verses. I'll never forget what one man said to me, "Our disappointments are sometimes God's appointments." It actually made me angry and hurt that someone would give me such a shallow response thinking it would be helpful.

In reading through the book of Job, we find an amazing story of one person's faithfulness to God, even when things had fallen apart. Job was learning an important lesson that we also need to learn: "I can't; God can—and I'll allow God to do so!" Job faced real issues (12:1–13:12). Job asked honest questions (13:13-28). And Job found "the answers" (Job 14–15).

*Encouragement from Scripture*

And he said to man, "The fear of the LORD—that is wisdom, and to shun evil is understanding." (Job 28:28)

*My response as I claim God's promises and grow stronger*

When was a time that I felt that friends let me down? What are some real issues I have faced in times of crisis? How did God help me through these difficult times?

*Practical steps that I will take today*

Today I will remember that healing takes time—lots of time and I won't rush that healing.

*My prayer*

I know I can't, but you can, and I'll let you, O God.

*Now I will take some moments to rest with God.*

Date     Thoughts / Feelings / Insight Gained / Prayer

_____

_____

_____

_____

_____

## 33 Today with God's help: I will remember that though my feelings change, God never changes

*Encouragement from experience*

Sometimes we get *really* mixed up. Our feelings change and we simply find ourselves unable to cope. A humorous story is told of an elderly woman frantically calling her husband on his cell phone. The frantic wife said, "Honey, I just heard on the news that some crazy man is driving the wrong way on the freeway, please be careful!" The man replied to his wife, "It's not just *one* car driving the wrong way honey, there's hundreds of them!"

Sometimes we simply cannot understand why God would permit something to come into our life, but God knows. Job felt abandoned because of what had happened (16:1-17), but he also felt anticipation for what was ahead (17:10-16). We may feel abandoned at times, but God is there. God is always there for us.

*Encouragement from Scripture*

I know that my Redeemer lives, and that in the end he will stand upon the earth. And after my skin has been destroyed, yet in my flesh I will see God; I myself will see him with my own eyes—I, and not another. How my heart yearns within me! (Job 19:25-27)

*My response as I claim God's promises and grow stronger*

When was a time I felt really abandoned? How did God keep me safe? How did God use others to help me during that time of crisis? When was the last time I felt someone was just "saying words" and not really being helpful? What were some learning experiences that helped me grow even though I felt abandonment? How has God comforted me since that time?

*Practical steps that I will take today*

Today I will cheer myself on. I will not dwell on regrets, and I will not fear failure. Today I will remember that healing takes time—lots of time. I will thank God for a new day.

*My prayer*

Lord, once again I need your gentle reminder that, though my feelings do change, you never change. Thank you for being there every day, all the time.

*Now I will take some moments to rest with God.*

*My spiritual healing journal*

Date    Thoughts / Feelings / Insight Gained / Prayer

_____

_____

_____

_____

_____

# 34 Today with God's help: I will learn about the "great tug of war" and gain victory

*Encouragement from experience*

Remember when you were a child and you used to play tug of war? Sometimes you could find two ropes and tie a knot in the middle to form four ends and play four-way tug-of-war. There was pulling, grasping, straining, and trying hard to win.

Job was in a tug-of-war. "Why do godly people suffer?" "How can I benefit from this suffering?" Job was a godly man whose life had fallen apart. His three friends were no help at all. Eliphaz offered dry theology; Bildad and Zophar gave him simple dogmatism. Job faced the issues, asked the questions, and found some "answers." Job learned that "feelings change but God doesn't." Job began his search and learned to let go. We may not understand God or God's ways, but it is always very important to trust God and God's sovereign guidance, even in life's tug of wars.

*Encouragement from Scripture*

In the land of Uz there lived a man whose name was Job. This man was blameless and upright; he feared God and shunned evil. (Job 1:1)

In all this, Job did not sin by charging God with wrongdoing. (Job 1:22)

*My response as I claim God's promises and grow stronger*

What are your real and honest doubts today? What do I need to turn over to God, in faith, today?

*Practical steps that I will take today*

Today I will acknowledge and accept that life pulls me in many different directions, and I cannot do everything. I will take a walk, go to a spa, have a good talk, or do some physical exercise. I will remember that healing takes time—lots of time.

*My prayer*

God power and majesty, grant me victory in life's tug of wars. Strengthen my faith.

*Now I will take some moments to rest with God.*

*My spiritual healing journal*

Date        Thoughts / Feelings / Insight Gained / Prayer

_____

_____

_____

_____

_____

# 35 Today with God's help: I will let God help me "go for the gold"

*Encouragement from experience*

I met with a family some years ago whose father passed away. As I listened to each family member share about this special man, I found out that the deceased man had won a gold medal. It was fascinating to hear family members share that this man's life's goal was literally to go for the gold. His desire was not to be second or third but first.

Job went for the gold! Job was a godly man whose life had fallen apart. Friends let him down, but God was still there. From his friends Job heard empty words and shallow answers. He heard superficial dogmatism. He was in a search for God alone. Job came forth as gold (23:10). This is sometimes true in our own lives. In Job 25–31 we read that Job learned of God's unlimited power and God's unlimited protection, at least ultimately.

### Encouragement from Scripture

I press on toward the goal to win the prize for which God has called me heavenward in Christ Jesus. (Philippians 3:14)

To him who is able to keep you from falling and to present you before his glorious presence without fault and with great joy— to the only God our Savior be glory, majesty, power and authority, through Jesus Christ our Lord, before all ages, now and forevermore! Amen. (Jude 24-25)

### My response as I claim God's promises and grow stronger

What has God called me to do today, for his glory? Will I do that? Am I more aware each day of God's power and protection?

### Practical steps that I will take today

Today I will understand my human limitations, I will be careful to watch out for burnout, but I *will* go for God's very best in my life. I will remember that healing takes time—lots of time.

### My prayer

Help me to trust fully in you and you alone, even in times of doubt and even when my life seems to be falling apart. I want to go for the gold and be your winner, Lord.

### Now I will take some moments to rest with God.

Date    Thoughts / Feelings / Insight Gained / Prayer

_____

_____

_____

_____

_____

## 36 Today with God's help: I will gain strength even though I may feel weak

*Encouragement from experience*

I've always been amazed watching constructions workers build skyscrapers. I am particularly impressed with how long it takes to build the foundation, but then I remember if the foundation is strong, the building will be strong. Years ago when I was a student in Chicago, I watched construction workers build the John Hancock building. What impressed me was how long they took to build the foundation. It seemed to me that it took as long or longer for them to build the foundation than it did to build the entire skyscraper!

Foundations are important in life. Sometimes God spends a great deal of time molding us for the future. One thing is certain—God knows exactly what is necessary to make us strong. We all go through difficult times, and it is important to gain strength from God. The prophet Isaiah and the psalmist wrote about the strength we can receive from the Lord.

For I am the LORD, your God, who takes hold of your right hand and says to you, Do not fear; I will help you. (Isaiah 41:13)

I life up my eyes to the hills—
    from where will my help come?
My help comes from the LORD,
    Who made heaven and earth.

He will not let your foot be moved;
    he who keeps you will not slumber.
He who keeps Israel
    will neither slumber nor sleep.

The LORD is your keeper;
    the LORD is your shade at your right hand.
        (Psalm 121:1-5; NRSV)

*My response as I claim God's promises and grow stronger*

In what area of my life do I need God's special strength today?

*Practical steps that I will take today*

Today I will trust in God and let God begin to help me rebuild dreams. Today I will accept the fact that sometimes it is difficult to give thanks, but I will give thanks today. I will remember that healing takes time—lots of time.

*My prayer*

God, my helper, I claim your strength today. I thank you for always being with me. Help me to give thanks at all times

*Now I will take some moments to rest with God.*

Date     Thoughts / Feelings / Insight Gained / Prayer

_____

_____

_____

_____

_____

## 37 Today with God's help: I will let God win the unknown battles in my life

*Encouragement from experience*

My associate's wife has leukemia. Over the years I've watched their relationship between her and her husband. They are very close; they've been married for many years and have given a wonderful testimony of God's goodness. But the roller coaster of good news and bad news has been a tremendous challenge. She was in and out of the hospital and back and forth to specialists and emergency rooms. These experiences have taught them to let God win the unknown battles in their lives. In Joshua 2:24 we read that God promised Joshua that the land of Canaan would be theirs. In Joshua 2 we see how God helped the spies win the battle of the unknown. We can apply that to our life as God helps us win our unknown battles. The spies were dispatched (v. 1); the spies were protected (vv. 2-7); the spies were informed about the unknown (vv. 8-11); and the spies promised Rahab safety (vv. 12-22). Finally the spies reported back (vv. 23, 24). Joshua let God win the unknown battles he was facing. What a great reminder for us today.

For the LORD your God is God in heaven above and on the earth below. (Joshua 2:11)

*My response as I claim God's promises and grow stronger*

What can I do to help ensure the salvation of my family? What "scarlet thread" (or lifeline) will I hold out, and hold onto, for life?

*Practical steps that I will take today*

Today I will accept the fact that life is not perfect and is filled with many unknowns. I will remember that healing takes time—lots of time.

*My prayer*

God, there are so many unknowns in my life right now. I need your help. I remember that you are an awesome God, who is in control. I give you the battles that are before me.

*Now I will take some moments to rest with God.*

*My spiritual healing journal*

Date     Thoughts / Feelings / Insight Gained / Prayer

_____

_____

_____

_____

_____

# 38 Today with God's help: I will thank God for victory over depression

*Encouragement from experience*

All of us go through a little depression once and a while. But a number of years ago, my wife experienced a prolonged time when she just could not shake off the feelings of depression. Depression seemed to grip her deeper each day until she found herself sitting alone in our bedroom all day, every day. The doctor had no idea how to solve the problem. A wonderful Christian counselor told us it was just the build-up of the exhaustion of helping others—what we sometimes call "burnout."

Depression is a loss of pleasure and enjoyment of life. It is feelings of sadness, disappointment, and loneliness. Sometimes it causes us to withdraw from people and activities. At some time or another, everyone experiences some depression. Sometimes depression lingers on; you can't seem to get back up or shake it off.

In Psalms 42 and 43 David did several things as he faced depression. He remembered how God had helped him in the past (42:4, 6). He practiced hope and praise, even during times of discouragement (42:5, 11; 43:5). He knew that God was his stronghold and his strength (43:2). He longed for God to guide him (43:3). And he went to God to find joy and delight (43:4).

*Encouragement from Scripture*

> Why are you downcast, O my soul?
>   and are you disquieted within me?
> Hope in God; for I shall again praise him,
>   my help and my God. (Psalm 42:5-6; NRSV)

So then, just as you received Christ Jesus as Lord, continue to live in him, rooted and built up in him, strengthened in the faith as you were taught, and overflowing with thankfulness. (Colossians 2:6-7)

*My response as I claim God's promises and grow stronger*

What causes God to seem far away at times? Who moved?

*Practical steps that I will take today*

Today I will persist in hope. I will seek godly counsel. I will trust in the Lord and ask God for strength. I will let God use others to help me. I will remember that healing takes time—lots of time.

*My prayer*

I pray that you will grant me victory and help me to trust in you fully.

*Now I will take some moments to rest with God.*

*My spiritual healing journal*

Date     Thoughts / Feelings / Insight Gained / Prayer

_____

_____

_____

_____

_____

# 39 Today with God's help: I will let God take over in my life

*Encouragement from experience*

I was driving to my office one morning and came to a group of quail trying to cross the street. It was quite humorous as I drove up to a crosswalk and stopped. There was a mother quail at the head and a long line of tiny baby quail following, and there came the daddy bringing up the tail. I couldn't help but grin as I saw this straight line of quail—I could almost hear the mother and father shouting to the little ones. They were concerned about safety I am sure, but they were teaching important lessons of life.

Control can be good or bad. Too much control hurts us and hurts people around us. We live in a society that is very controlling. We like to be in charge of things. Sometimes it is difficult in our spiritual life, to just let go and let God take over for us. The apostle Paul wrote that we must learn to give our lives to God as a "sacrifice," which means that God is in control. Sometimes that is difficult to do.

*Encouragement from Scripture*

Therefore, I urge you, brothers [and sisters], in view of God's mercy, to offer your bodies as living sacrifices, holy and pleasing to God—this is your spiritual act of worship. Do not conform any longer to the pattern of this world, but be transformed by the renewing of your mind. Then you will be able to test and approve what God's will is—his good, pleasing and perfect will. (Romans 12:1-2)

*My response as I claim God's promises and grow stronger*

In what area of my life is God inviting me to hand over control? What is my response to that?

Today I will read God's Word and let God work in and through me. I will make a conscious decision to become a living sacrifice to God. I will remember that healing takes time—lots of time.

*My prayer*

I let you take control of every area of my life today, Lord. I give thanks.

*Now I will take some moments to rest with God.*

*My spiritual healing journal*

Date      Thoughts / Feelings / Insight Gained / Prayer

_____

_____

_____

_____

_____

## 40 Today with God's help: I will have confidence because of God and God's grace in my life

*Encouragement from experience*

A lot of things in life make us feel insecure. As human beings we may tend to lack confidence, but as believers, as Christians, we have confidence because of God's grace in our lives.

When I was a first year theological student in Chicago, I learned a lot about life in the big city, and I learned much about safety and confidence. I loved to walk the streets of the city of Chicago, but I quickly learned that there are many dangers in an urban area. I watched the police stop people and make arrests. I saw intoxicated persons on the street. As a young student, I witnessed violence. One thing I remember especially clearly: as I would walk back to school along La Salle Street, I would come to a huge arch that was the entry to the school. Every time I walked through that arch, I felt the security of coming home. That arch was a place of safety.

When we are hurt physically, we lose confidence. After surgery, we find it difficult to make ourselves move an arm, leg, or other part of our body. Why? Because it hurts. Emotional and spiritual healing requires that we regain confidence as well. But with God's help and in God's strength, we can heal.

### Encouragement from Scripture

And this is the testimony: God has given us eternal life, and this life is in his Son. He who has the Son has life; he who does not have the Son of God does not have life. I write these things to you who believe in the name of the Son of God so that you may know that you have eternal life. This is the confidence we have in approaching God: that if we ask anything according to his will, he hears us. And if we know that he hears us—whatever we ask—we know that we have what we asked of him. (1 John 5:11-15)

### My response as I claim God's promises and grow stronger

In what area of my life do I need confidence today? What do I need to ask God for today?

### Practical steps that I will take today

Today I will not fear failure, but I will let God build my emotional and spiritual confidence for God's own glory. I will remember that healing takes time—lots of time.

*My prayer*

Loving God, give me the confidence that I need for this day.

*Now I will take some moments to rest with God.*

*My spiritual healing journal*

Date        Thoughts / Feelings / Insight Gained / Prayer

_____

_____

_____

_____

_____


# 41 | Today with God's help: I will accept my mistakes and move on

*Encouragement from experience*

I chuckled when I heard a bride tell me that in haste she wrote generic thank-you notes to everyone who gave them a gift at their wedding. Her generic note read, "thank you for the lovely gift, we plan to use it real soon." Unfortunately, the gift one particular person had given was a fire extinguisher!

We make mistakes and that's just a part of life. All too often we are in too much of a rush. God often wants to teach us lessons during difficult times. We must not rush ahead of God. We must learn the lessons that God wants to teach us, even during the difficult times of life. From the human perspective many things seem impossible. But with God, nothing is impossible. (See Mark 10:27.) Think of it—God is on our side. God is sovereign. God always knows what is ahead and is there for us, even when things look bleak. Even when I make mistakes! When I blow it, God is there to lead me back on course.

*Encouragement from Scripture*

Jesus looked at them and said, "For mortals it is impossible, but not for God; for God all things are possible." (Mark 10:27)

The LORD is near to all who call on him,
    to all who call on him in truth.
He fulfills the desires of all who fear him;
    he also hears their cry, and saves them.
        (Psalm 145:18-19; NRSV)

*My response as I claim God's promises and grow stronger*

What mistakes have I made in recent days? How did God step in to bring me back on course?

*Practical steps that I will take today*

Today I will review my personal priorities and make any needed changes. I will remember that healing takes time—lots of time.

*My prayer*

I thank you God for your loving guidance in my life. Thank you, that even when I make mistakes, you are there. You accept me and help me to move ahead.

*Now I will take some moments to rest with God.*

Date     Thoughts / Feelings / Insight Gained / Prayer

_____

_____

_____

_____

_____

# 42 Today with God's help: I know that my future is bright

*Encouragement from experience*

Who could ever forget that morning of September 11, 2001, when two planes crashed into the twin towers in New York? Or the bombings we read about in the daily newspapers? Or the crime that seems to have taken over our cities? If we only read the newspaper, listen to the news, and watch reports on television, we think the future is dim. But the future is bright if we know God and God's love. With our world filled with violence, it is difficult to think that there is a bright future—but there is! Remember that God is sovereign. We have a bright future because of God's love for us. Instead of just reading today's newspaper, try reading some Scripture right before reading the paper. You may be amazed at the new perspective you will have.

*Encouragement from Scripture*

You show me the path of life.
   In your presence there is fullness of joy;
   In your right hand are pleasures forevermore.
      (Psalm 16:11)

Rejoice in the Lord always. I will say it again: Rejoice! Let your gentleness be evident to all. The Lord is near. (Philippians 4:4-5)

> He leads the humble in what is right,
>> and teaches the humble his way.
> All the paths of the LORD are steadfast love and faithfulness,
>> for those who keep his covenant and his decrees.
>> (Psalm 25:9-10; NRSV)

"For I know the plans I have for you," declares the LORD, "plans to prosper you and not to harm you, plans to give you hope and a future. Then you will call upon me and come and pray to me, and I will listen to you. You will seek me and find me when you seek me with all your heart." (Jeremiah 29:11-13)

### My response as I claim God's promises and grow stronger

How do I feel as I realize that wherever my path goes, God is going ahead of me? What does God want me to do today? Where does God want me to go today?

### Practical steps that I will take today

Today I will make the decision to remain/become active in worship in a local congregation. I will worship God alone in a quiet time, but I will also worship God with others on a regular basis. I will remember that healing takes time—lots of time.

### My prayer

I thank you for the future that is bright because of you.

### Now I will take some moments to rest with God.

Date      Thoughts / Feelings / Insight Gained / Prayer

_____

_____

_____

_____

_____

## 43 Today with God's help: I will serve God and share God's love

*Encouragement from experience*

My parents were humble people with little earthly means. They worked hard all during their life together, and in their closing days on earth, they divided their meager estate between their children. Each portion was a very small financial amount, but the mementos and personal items were priceless.

We will share in God's inheritance. That is an amazing truth. Paul writes in Colossians that God has "qualified" us to share in the inheritance of the saints in the kingdom of light. That's something to get excited about. That's something that makes us want to serve God and share God's love. Today, with God's help—I will serve God and share God's love

*Encouragement from Scripture*

And we pray this in order that you may live a life worthy of the Lord and may please him in every way: bearing fruit in every good work, growing in the knowledge of God, being strengthened with all power according to his glorious might so that you may have great endurance and patience, and joyfully giving thanks to the Father, who has qualified you to share in the inheritance of the saints in the kingdom of light. (Colossians 1:10-12)

*My response as I claim God's promises and grow stronger*

To whom will I talk to today about God's love? What comes to my mind when I hear the phrase "qualified to share in the inheritance of the saints in the kingdom of light"?

*Practical steps that I will take today*

Today I will accept the reality that I need help, but others need help too. I will reach out to someone else and try to help. I will remember that healing takes time—lots of time.

*My prayer*

How I thank you, God, for my inheritance in the kingdom that is yet to come.

*Now I will take some moments to rest with God.*

*My spiritual healing journal*

Date        Thoughts / Feelings / Insight Gained / Prayer

_____

_____

_____

_____

_____

# 44 Today with God's help: I will let God be my deliverer

*Encouragement from experience*

I served on the board of a nonprofit neighborhood action program center in Phoenix, Arizona. Each month I saw its financial situation getting worse and the point drawing nearer when they could easily be faced with closing the doors of the center. That day came, and for three or four days the center was closed, and there were many hurting people left in an even more desperate situation. The next Sunday evening I went to our congregation and shared from my heart the great need that existed, only about an hour's drive from where we were all sitting so comfortably. I had no prepared notes, and I really didn't plan to receive an offering. After I shared, a man raised his hand and suggested we receive an offering. Others agreed so we placed some offering plates at the back. A miracle took place that night. It was a small crowd but God touched hearts and over four thousand dollars was placed in the offering plates. With God's help that neighborhood action center opened its doors Monday morning. When I handed the director the offering he sat in his chair and wept. Emotional and spiritual victories are gained only in and through the power of God.

The psalmist wrote about needy people (Psalm 40). The psalmist reminds us that God is our help and our deliverer (v. 17). It is important to call on God for help and strength in times of need. It is also important to thank God and to give God thanks and praise for divine (and earthly!) goodness.

*Encouragement from Scripture*

> As for me, I am poor and needy,
>> But the Lord takes thought for me.
> You are my help and my deliverer;
>> do not delay, O my God. (Psalm 40:17; NRSV)

Cast all your anxiety on him because he cares for you. (1 Peter 5:7)

How weighty[3] to me are your thoughts, O God!
   How vast is the sum of them!
I try to count them—they are more than the sand;
   I awake[4]—I am still with you. (Psalm 139:17-18; NRSV)

*My response as I claim God's promises and grow stronger*

Looking back over my life, how has God been my faithful deliverer? What is my response to the fact that God is always with me?

*Practical steps that I will take today*

Today I will allow myself to let friends help me. I will listen to godly friends and how they see that I perceive any loss I feel in my life. I will remember that healing takes time—lots of time.

*My prayer*

I thank and praise you for being my deliverer, O God. Accept my praise O God.

*Now I will take some moments to rest with God.*

*My spiritual healing journal*

Date      Thoughts / Feelings / Insight Gained / Prayer

_____

_____

_____

---

[3] NIV: "precious."

[4] "I awake" is the alternate NRSV translation and agrees with the NIV translation. NRSV's first translation is "I come to the end."

## 45 Today with God's help: I will be released from worry and anxiety, and I will remember how much God cares for me

*Encouragement from experience*

I have a friend who loves to worry. I guess we all do that some-times, but this person goes out of her way to worry. You can pray with her, she can share her burdens, and you can give great sug-gestions or solutions—but she will just keep right on worrying. She has never allowed herself the freedom of just letting go and letting God handle her situations. It's so easy to carry around a bag of worry. We allow ourselves to "wallow in self-pity."

The First Letter of Peter reminds us that we are to cast off our anxiety. Peter gives us the reason as well; he says we are to cast off our anxiety because God cares for us.

*Encouragement from Scripture*

Cast all your anxiety on him because he cares for you. (1 Peter 5:7)

Cast your burden on the LORD,
    and he will sustain you;
he will never permit
    the righteous to be moved. (Psalm 55:22; NRSV)

*My response as I claim God's promises and grow stronger*

What is in my "bag of worry"? How long have I been carry-ing around that worry bag? What does God want me to do with that right now?

Today I will cast off my anxiety and constantly remind myself that God really does care for me. I will enjoy some good times with others, and I will remember that healing takes time—lots of time.

*My prayer*

Give me strength right now, God, to toss off any worry and anxiety that is in my life. Remind me of your loving care.

*Now I will take some moments to rest with God.*

*My spiritual healing journal*

Date     Thoughts / Feelings / Insight Gained / Prayer

_____

_____

_____

_____

_____

## 46 Today with God's help: I will remember that Jesus is interceding for me

*Encouragement from experience*

We have two young granddaughters ages two and four. When they were younger, I found it difficult to understand what the youngest child was trying to tell me. I was amazed at her mom being able to understand exactly what she was saying. The reason is that special relationship between mom and child. That mom had a bond that no one else had with that child.

It is something like that with the Holy Spirit and Jesus. Jesus intercedes for me in prayer. It is a wonderful thought to realize that God's Son, Jesus, is actually in heaven right now interceding for me and my needs. When I pray, Jesus intercedes. When I present a request in prayer, Jesus presents that to God the Father. Paul writes about that wonderful process in Romans 8. Paul also gives us great encouragement in reminding us that nothing will separate us from God's love.

### Encouragement from Scripture

Christ Jesus, who died—more than that, who was raised to life—is at the right hand of God and is also interceding for us. Who shall separate us from the love of Christ? Shall trouble or hardship or persecution or famine or nakedness or danger or sword? As it is written: "For your sake we face death all day long; we are considered as sheep to be slaughtered." No, in all these things we are more than conquerors through him who loved us. For I am convinced that neither death nor life, neither angels nor demons, neither the present nor the future, nor any powers, neither height nor depth, nor anything else in all creation, will be able to separate us from the love of God that is in Christ Jesus our Lord. (Romans 8:36-39)

### My response as I claim God's promises and grow stronger

How have difficulties and hardships affected my emotional and spiritual life? When was the last time I thanked God for the Holy Spirit's power of intercession on my behalf?

### Practical steps that I will take today

Today I will become better informed about God's wonderful promises. I will reflect on God's goodness all day long. I will remember that healing takes time—lots of time.

*My prayer*

Thank you for interceding for me. I love you, God.

*Now I will take some moments to rest with God.*

*My spiritual healing journal*

Date      Thoughts / Feelings / Insight Gained / Prayer

_____

_____

_____

_____

_____

# 47 Today with God's help: I will rejoice in God's strength

*Encouragement from experience*

I've gone to a gym, YMCA, or fitness center for physical exercise nearly all of my adult life. One thing that is certain: if there are others working out, I am greatly encouraged and do a much better job. I am motivated by others.

Question: How strong have you become emotionally and spiritually in your spiritual journey? Is it time to let the joy of God be your strength?

Nehemiah learned that great lesson. Though he was faced with a lot of problems, he took them to God in prayer, and he found joy in God.

*Encouragement from Scripture*

Nehemiah said, "For the joy of the LORD is your strength." (Nehemiah 8:10)

*My response as I claim God's promises and grow stronger*

When was I physically hurting? What caused that? How was that healed? When was I emotionally or spiritually hurting? What caused that? How has that been healed? What will I do today to put into practice the reality that the joy of the Lord is my strength?

*Practical steps that I will take today*

Today I will cultivate a joyful attitude. I will rejoice and say, "This *is* the day that the LORD has made." I will remember that healing takes time—lots of time.

*My prayer*

Like Nehemiah, Lord, hear My prayer that you are my joy and my strength.

*Now I will take some moments to rest with God.*

*My spiritual healing journal*

Date     Thoughts / Feelings / Insight Gained / Prayer

_____

_____

_____

_____

_____

# 48 Today with God's help: I will thank God for the Holy Spirit

*Encouragement from experience*

In January 2001, I had the opportunity to make a spiritual pilgrimage to the Holy Land with a group of pastors. An incident in the Garden of Gethsemane touched me deeply. We were all around the olive trees where Jesus had prayed that night before his crucifixion. As we all began to leave I noticed one pastor sitting under the old olive tree weeping. I left him in his private time with the Lord, but later he saw me at a distance and motioned for me to come over to him. He spoke these words, "Oh, how I thank God for sending his Son Jesus."

In Romans 8, the apostle Paul tells us that the Holy Spirit is with us always. When you know Jesus Christ as your savior, the Holy Spirit dwells within you. You are God's child and the Holy Spirit gives you strength.

*Encouragement from Scripture*

In the same way, the Spirit helps us in our weakness. We do not know what we ought to pray for, but the Spirit himself intercedes for us with groans that words cannot express. And he who searches our hearts knows the mind of the Spirit, because the Spirit intercedes for the saints in accordance with God's will. And we know that in all things God works for the good of those who love him, who have been called according to his purpose. (Romans 8:26-28)

*My response as I claim God's promises and grow stronger*

In what ways am I weak today? How can God help me in that weakness?

*Practical steps that I will take today*

Today I will thank God for the Holy Spirit. I will not fear the future, realizing that God is in full control and that the Holy Spirit empowers me daily. I will remember that healing takes time—lots of time.

*My prayer*

I claim the Holy Spirit's power for my life today, Lord.

*Now I will take some moments to rest with God.*

*My spiritual healing journal*

Date      Thoughts / Feelings / Insight Gained / Prayer

_____

_____

_____

_____

_____

# 49 Today with God's help: I will praise the Lord with all my heart

(See Psalm 9:1.)

*Encouragement from experience*

In my former congregation we had a large number of families and young adults. As in many congregations, we had two worship services: one was traditional and one was contemporary. By contemporary I mean that we had a "praise team" who led us in worship and praise to God; there were drums, guitars, and a small ensemble orchestra. It was not very funny at the time, but looking back now it is rather humorous: One man in the church came to me and respectfully said, "Pastor, I cannot worship the Lord seeing those drums from the first service up there." I told him not to worry, that it would be taken care of by the next Sunday. I asked our worship team leader to just put a cover over them to keep them safe. The next Sunday after our second service the man came to me again and said that he could still not worship because he "saw" the drums up there with the cover over them! I said that the situation would be resolved by the next Sunday, and I simply asked the worship team to pull the drums off to the side after the first service. The third Sunday the man came to me and said, "Pastor, I just can't worship the Lord knowing those drums are in that side room!"

Praise is a wonderful word but praise comes from the heart. Praise is internally expressing what is going on inside of our heart. Praise opens us up and gives us release. Praise exalts the name of our Lord and pleases God. Praise is good medicine—as is laughter. It is important to give thanks. It is important to lift praise up to God.

*Encouragement from Scripture*

> Blessed be the Lord,
>> who daily bears us up;
>> God is our salvation. (Psalm 68:19)

> Enter his gates with thanksgiving
>> and his courts with praise.
>> Give thanks to him, bless his name.

> For the LORD is good;
>> his steadfast love endures forever,
>> and his faithfulness to all generations.
>>> (Psalm 100:4-5; NRSV)

Through Jesus, therefore, let us continually offer to God a sacrifice of praise—the fruit of lips that confess his name. (Hebrews 13:15)

*My response as I claim God's promises and grow stronger*

How has God taken my burdens and given me peace today? What will I do today to express my love for God and God's goodness to me?

*Practical steps that I will take today*

Today I will praise God all day long. I will give thanks. I will acknowledge that God daily carries my burdens and I will be thankful. I will remember that healing takes time—lots of time.

*My prayer*

Help me to truly praise you, Father. Accept my praise.

*Now I will take some moments to rest with God.*

*My spiritual healing journal*

Date       Thoughts / Feelings / Insight Gained / Prayer

_____

_____

_____

_____

_____

# 50 Today with God's help: I will thank God for sending the only Son, Jesus

*Encouragement from experience*

I have a little gold key chain that was given to me by my daughter when she was a child. I've kept that key chain over the years, and (of course!) it is a wonderful reminder every day, all day long, of the precious bond between dad and daughter. Gifts are wonderful, especially personal gifts. When God sent his Son Jesus to this world, it was an extremely personal act. Jesus came for you! He came that you might live.

*Encouragement from Scripture*

For God so loved the world that he gave his one and only Son, that whoever believes in him shall not perish but have eternal life. For God did not send his Son into the world to condemn the world, but to save the world through him. Whoever believes in him is not condemned, but whoever does not believe stands condemned already because he has not believed in the name of God's one and only Son. (John 3:16-18)

This is how God showed his love among us: He sent his one and only Son into the world that we might live through him. (1 John 4:9)

*My response as I claim God's promises and grow stronger*

What might I do today that will show God how much I want to express love in return? Who needs to hear about God's love today? How will I share God's love with that person?

*Practical steps that I will take today*

Today I will make a telephone call to a friend and encourage him or her. I will tell them of God's love, and I will thank God for sending Jesus. I will remember that healing takes time—lots of time.

*My prayer*

Oh, God, I thank you for sending your Son Jesus to be my Savior.

*Now I will take some moments to rest with God.*

*My spiritual healing journal*

Date        Thoughts / Feelings / Insight Gained / Prayer

_____

_____

_____

_____

_____

# 51 | Today with God's help: I will set some new goals for my life

*Encouragement from experience*

Some years ago my wife and I had the opportunity to see the musical Annie when it was playing in Los Angeles at the Pantageous Theater. It was an affirmation of life. Little Orphan Annie gave hope and positive expectations to everyone with enthusiastic singing of the theme song "Tomorrow." When we left the musical, the words lingered in our minds. Odd, isn't it, how a simple song of hope can lift people out of discouragement with life's troubles and give assurance of a new beginning? You are coming to the end of a journey and yet it is really not the end but the beginning. You set a goal to journey through this meditation book. Now you come to the close of that journey. You may repeat this journey "in a new place" as many times as you wish.

It is time to set some new goals. In 1 Thessalonians we read that the God of peace sanctifies us (or sets us apart). As you come to the end of this journey, it is important to realize that your journey is actually just beginning. Now it is time to grow stronger in the Lord, which may mean giving God our weakness. (See 2 Corinthians 12:1-10.)

*Encouragement from Scripture*

May God himself, the God of peace, sanctify you through and through. May your whole spirit, soul and body be kept blameless at the coming of our Lord Jesus Christ. The one who calls you is faithful and he will do it. (1 Thessalonians 5:23-24)

*My response as I claim God's promises and grow stronger*

What does God desire for my goals right now? How can I show my love for God and for God's faithfulness?

*Practical steps that I will take today*

Today I will set some new goals for myself with God's direction. I will find a support group with Christian friends to help me grow. I will remember that healing takes time—lots of time.

*My prayer*

Help me, God, to set the goals for my life that *you* desire.

*Now I will take some moments to rest with God.*

Date    Thoughts / Feelings / Insight Gained / Prayer

_____

_____

_____

_____

_____

# 52 Today with God's help: I will thank God for this spiritual journey

*Encouragement from experience*

I guess I've been with hundreds of people who were experiencing difficult times. I have noticed the difference of how people respond to pain and suffering. Some become very bitter and others allow that pain and suffering to make them a better person. Suffering and glory is a theme in the Scriptures. Jesus suffered when he went to the cross, but after he arose there was glory. He is now seated at the right hand of God the Father. Until we are in heaven, God has given us the Holy Spirit to dwell within us to help us, strengthen us, and comfort us. Looking back at your experience before and during your spiritual journey with this meditation book, think of what suffering you have gone through, but then remember the glory that is to come. Reflect on the suffering of Jesus and thank God for the glory that is ahead in heaven.

*Encouragement from Scripture*

The Spirit himself testifies with our spirit that we are God's children. Now if we are children, then we are heirs—heirs of

God and co-heirs with Christ, if indeed we share in his sufferings in order that we may also share in his glory. I consider that our present sufferings are not worth comparing with the glory that will be revealed in us. (Romans 8:16-18)

*My response as I claim God's promises and grow stronger*

What can I say to God to express my deep heartfelt appreciation for the divine love?

*Practical steps that I will take today*

Today I will thank God for the past days of this spiritual journey. I will claim the Holy Spirit's power in my life. I will remember the suffering of Jesus and thank God for the glory that is ahead for me in heaven. I have learned that healing takes time—lots of time.

*My prayer*

Help me to be thankful every day of my life, thankful for your goodness in my life.

*Now I will take some moments to rest with God.*

*My spiritual healing journal*

Date    Thoughts / Feelings / Insight Gained / Prayer

_____

_____

_____

_____

_____

*Here are eight additional meditations and reflections—with power thoughts in each day—to give you added strength and encouragement when you are feeling desperate. There is also a list of resources to help you in times of crisis and times of need.*

## Today with God's help: I will thank God for blessing those who mourn

*Encouragement from experience*

Power thoughts: Feelings of purposelessness are very normal, but everything *does* have a purpose even though we do not see that purpose at the moment. My feelings of weakness are all part of the grief and bereavement process. Never give up.

I had just gone through a very difficult time in my life. I was struggling to gain victory. I knew that God was there, but I kept wondering: "where?" Why didn't God stop the pain? One evening, I went for a walk to pray and gain victory. It seemed as though the further I walked the deeper the pain grew in my heart and soul. Finally, I could stand it no more and I stopped at a large rock by the road and sat on it and cried out in agony: "O God, I don't know how much more pain I can take!" That release seemed to give God the opportunity he was waiting for. God was waiting for me to let go and let him take my pain. After all, God took my sin on the cross. God promised to carry my burden. I gave it to God at that moment, and I began to heal. In Matthew 5:4, Jesus gives a special blessing to those who are hurting. Today I will think about that blessing. Today I will reflect on how mourning affects me personally.

Mourning affects my relationship with God and brings me to forgiveness and humility. Mourning affects me personally, and it affects my attitudes and actions. Mourning affects my relationship with others around me.

*Encouragement from Scripture*

Blessed are those who mourn, for they will be comforted. (Matthew 5:4)

*My response as I claim God's promises and grow stronger*

When was a time when I was mourning? What was a source of encouragement and comfort to me during that time?

*Practical steps that I will take today*

Today I will be reminded that crying can be cleansing and I will draw on my faith for healing. I will remember that healing takes time—lots of time.

*My prayer*

Thank you for reminding me of your blessing on those who are hurting. Give me strength for this day.

*Now I will take some moments to rest with God.*

*My spiritual healing journal*

Date      Thoughts / Feelings / Insight Gained / Prayer

_____

_____

_____

_____

_____

# 2 Today with God's help: I will acknowledge that God calms life's storms

*Encouragement from experience*

Power thoughts: We must accept our feelings of fear if we are to heal; fear is a very normal part of grief, loss, and bereavement. Others *do* feel the way we feel and others *do* care about us and our feelings.

Some years ago we were living in Santa Monica, California, and the Northridge earthquake hit early in the morning. I'll never forget being awakened from sleep hearing the crashing of dishes and furniture. My wife and I jumped out of bed and stood hugging each other in the doorway waiting for the quake to stop. For a few moments we really thought that was the "big one" that everyone had talked about for so many years. When the shaking stopped, we made our way through the rubble and stood outside on the street with hundreds of other frightened people. I found it amazing how strangers quickly began to bond together by simply telling their stories and sharing their fears.

Healing takes time, but it also takes other human beings to encourage and give comfort. In Mark 4:35-41 there is a story of Jesus calming the storm. Some practical biblical lessons are found there: Since Jesus is with me on my journey, I don't have to be afraid (vv. 35-36). Storms often come suddenly and severely (v. 37). Jesus wants to be the storm calmer in my life today (v. 38).

*Encouragement from Scripture*

That day when evening came, he said to his disciples, "Let us go over to the other side." Leaving the crowd behind, they took him along, just as he was, in the boat. There were also other boats with him. A furious squall came up, and the waves broke over the boat, so that it was nearly swamped. Jesus was in the stern, sleeping on a cushion. The disciples woke him and said to him, "Teacher, don't you care if we drown?" He got up, rebuked the wind and said to the waves, "Quiet! Be still!" Then the wind died down and it was completely calm. He said to his disciples, "Why are you so afraid? Do you still have no faith?" They were terrified and asked each other, "Who is this? Even the wind and the waves obey him!" (Mark 4:35-41)

*My response as I claim God's promises and grow stronger*

How do I react when Jesus seems to be asleep in my life?

*Practical steps that I will take today*

Today I will get the support that I need to help me face any storm that I may be facing today—or to face any storm that may be coming. I will remember that healing takes time—lots of time.

*My prayer*

Jesus, I know that you are the storm calmer. I ask you to calm my heart and to give me your peace today.

*Now I will take some moments to rest with God.*

*My spiritual healing journal*

Date      Thoughts / Feelings / Insight Gained / Prayer

_____

_____

_____

_____

_____

## 3 Today with God's help: I will learn about praying in times of trouble

*Encouragement from experience*

Power thoughts: Caring people *do* want to help; I need to allow others to help. There are caring people who do want to pray with me and give me guidance, encouragement, and strength.

We all need someone to listen to us, someone who really cares. Praying is talking to God. God listen, cares, and loves us. He sent Jesus to die on the cross for our sins. God listens and responds. People today desperately want someone to listen to them.

A friend of mine told me that he read an interesting ad in the newspaper one day that reminded him of just how desperate people today really are. The ad said that for $5.00 someone would listen to the caller for thirty minutes! Sometimes, in desperation, we will do anything to have just one person really listen to us. God is always ready and willing to listen. Sometimes we feel like the world is crushing in on us. We live in a world filled with trouble and fear. An old adage says, "Prayer changes things," but perhaps more accurately, prayer changes people. As I face this day, I will learn about praying in times of trouble.

*Encouragement from Scripture*

O Lord, how many are my foes!
    Many are rising against me;
many are saying to me,
    "There is no help for you in God."

But you, O Lord, are a shield around me,
    my glory, and the one who lifts up my head.
I cry aloud to the Lord,
    and he answers me from his holy hill.
I lie down and sleep;
    I wake again, for the Lord sustains me.

I am not afraid of ten thousands of people
  who have set themselves against me all around.

Rise up, O LORD!
  Deliver me, O my God!

. . . . . . . . . . . . . . . . . . . . . . . .

Deliverance belongs to the LORD;
  may your blessing be on your people! (Psalm 3; NRSV)

*My response as I claim God's promises and grow stronger*

What is the worst trouble I had this last week? Where did I go for help?

*Practical steps that I will take today*

Today I will let go and let God take over, I will let go and relax and I will let others help me. I will remember that healing takes time—lots of time.

*My prayer*

Teach me how to pray, O God, not just in times of trouble, but teach me to be praying all day long.

*Now I will take some moments to rest with God.*

*My spiritual healing journal*

Date      Thoughts / Feelings / Insight Gained / Prayer

_____

_____

_____

# 4 Today with God's help: I will grow in my faith during times of trials

*Encouragement from experience*

Power thoughts: Confusion is part of my healing, it is normal and it will get better. Even when the pain seems unbearable, God *is* there to help.

September 11, 2001, will be remembered forever as a defining moment in our history. We saw men and women of faith make incredible decisions. The words "Let's roll" are imprinted on our minds and hearts. Todd Beamer wasn't supposed to be on the United Airlines flight 93 that morning. He normally took a night flight. But Todd Beamer spent the night with family members and left early the next morning on flight 93. He was a person of faith. Just before the fatal crash he was talking on the plane's Airfone, and for some reason the call reached an operator. He gave the details, "Three hijackers, two with knives; ten passengers in first class; twenty-seven in coach, and five flight attendants." Their plan was to overthrow the hijackers. He asked the operator to pray with him. He prayed the Lord's Prayer and recited Psalm 23. The operator heard, "Jesus help me!" then, "Are you guys ready?" and finally "Let's roll." There were sounds of struggle and then silence! A family was left behind—but with God's help growing in strength together. His wife wrote a powerful book telling of God's strength through that experience. (*Let's Roll: Ordinary People, Extraordinary Courage* [Wheaton, IL.: Tyndale, 2002]).

*Encouragement from Scripture*

For the LORD your God is the one who goes with you to fight for you against your enemies to give you victory. (Deuteronomy 20:4)

The LORD is in his holy temple;
   the LORD's throne is in heaven.
   His eyes behold, his gaze examines humankind.
      (Psalm 11:4; NRSV)

*My response as I claim God's promises and grow stronger*

What has my faith cost me? How will I grow stronger through this experience?

*Practical steps that I will take today*

Today I will let others know of my needs and let them help me. I will help myself. I will remember that healing takes time—lots of time.

*My prayer*

Give me a strong faith today that I may live for you.

*Now I will take some moments to rest with God.*

*My spiritual healing journal*

Date      Thoughts / Feelings / Insight Gained / Prayer

_____

_____

_____

_____

_____

## 5 Today with God's help: I will remember that faith says to keep on

*Encouragement from experience*

Power thoughts: It is normal to lash out at others when hurt is present; it is also normal to feel that I am on an emotional roller coaster. It is okay to not be able to understand things. In fact, that too is very normal during times of loss, grief, and bereavement.

Winston Churchill was asked to give the commencement address at his alma mater. The auditorium was hot, and the program was painfully long. Churchill was finally introduced. He went to the podium and spoke twenty-nine words! "Never give in; never give in, never, never, never, never. In nothing great or small, large or petty, never give in, except in convictions of honor and good sense." As we claim God's promises, it is important to remember to press on, to keep going, even when it may be easier to give up. Never give up.

*Encouragement from Scripture*

Therefore, since we are surrounded by such a great cloud of witnesses, let us throw off everything that hinders and the sin that so easily entangles, and let us run with perseverance the race marked out for us. Let us fix our eyes on Jesus, the author and perfecter of our faith, who for the joy set before him endured the cross, scorning its shame, and sat down at the right hand of the throne of God. Consider him who endured such opposition from sinful men, so that you will not grow weary and lose heart. (Hebrews 12:1-3)

*My response as I claim God's promises and grow stronger*

When did I feel like quitting? How did God step in to give me courage to continue on?

*Practical steps that I will take today*

Today I will remember that healing and growth has progress and regress. I will accept my feelings even though I may not understand them. I will remember that healing takes time—lots of time.

*My prayer*

Help me to keep focused on you, God. Give me patience, and make me a stronger person as you guide my life this day.

*Now I will take some moments to rest with God.*

*My spiritual healing journal*

Date      Thoughts / Feelings / Insight Gained / Prayer

_____

_____

_____

_____

_____

## 6 Today with God's help: I will accept that there may be good in grief

*Encouragement from experience*

Power thoughts: Often it may seem that there is no light at the end of the tunnel, but God is there to help you through the darkness. God really does want to do a miracle in your life today—it is important to let God do that miracle.

About 4:00 A.M. I received a telephone call from the local hospital asking me to come to the intensive care to be with a man who was in an emergency. I went to pray with him and his wife. Numerous times over the days that followed I was called back to the hospital because doctors thought he was slipping away. Then one day when my cell phone rang, the nurse told me it would indeed by very soon. As I walked into the intensive-care unit my wife and I saw the man. His wife was by his bedside staring at the heart monitor, listening to beeps, and watching blood pressure numbers drop lower and lower. We all knew that it would be moments before his passing. Any pastor or caregiver who has been helping people with serious illness knows the deafening sound of the solid beep and the glaring, straight line on the monitor. He slipped away.

Could there be any good in this situation? Is there any good in that sort of grief? I'll never forget holding his wife's hand and hugging her as she wept. I have gone through experiences like this hundreds of times, and the pain I personally feel for the family members left behind has never lessened. After some time I whispered to her "He is gone—he is in the presence of the Lord," to which she shouted back at me, "No, don't say that; he is not gone. Call the nurses. Do something."

Psalm 91 says that good can be hidden within grief: when we understand that our feelings and our timelines differ . . . when we realize that the stages of grieving often blend together (v. 2) . . . when we remember that God is always with us and covers us (vv. 3-8) . . . when we let our grief open a door of opportunity to help someone else (vv. 9-12) . . . and when our grief helps us readjust our priorities to focus on God, God's Love, and God's Word (vv. 13-16).

*Encouragement from Scripture*

> You who live in the shelter of the Most High,
>     who abide in the shadow of the Almighty,
> will say to the LORD, "My refuge and my fortress;
>     my God, in whom I trust."

For he will deliver you from the snare of the fowler
and from the deadly pestilence;

. . . . . . . . . . . . . . . . . . . . .

Those who love me, I will deliver;
I will protect those who know my name.
When they call to me, I will answer them;
I will be with them in trouble,
I will rescue them and honor them.
With long life I will satisfy them,
and show them my salvation. (Psalm 91:1-3, 14-16; NRSV)

*My response as I claim God's promises and grow stronger*

What can I learn from the grief I have experienced?

*Practical steps that I will take today*

Today I will deal with and accept my feelings—and not blame someone else. Today I will remember that grief is not my enemy! I will remember that healing takes time—lots of time.

*My prayer*

Help me see the bigger picture that you see.

*Now I will take some moments to rest with God.*

*My spiritual healing journal*

Date       Thoughts / Feelings / Insight Gained / Prayer

_____

_____

_____

_____

_____

# 7 Today with God's help: I will acknowledge that sometimes life throws out some hardballs

*Encouragement from experience*

Power thoughts: The feeling of "will this ever end" is very normal and it is at that moment when you feel it will never end that God is right there to reach out to you in moments of desperation. Crises in life may be times of greatest growth and opportunities to not only heal but to actually allow you to help someone else.

I stand before people all the time and teach Scripture. I remember one Sunday morning teaching from Romans 8. I knew the passage well—academically. But God wanted me to put the verses into practice. In Romans 8:31-35 the apostle Paul asks five questions. "If God is for us, who can be against us?" (v. 31). "Don't you know that God will give you all things?" (v. 32). "[W]ho will bring any charge against those whom God has chosen?" (v. 33). "Who is he that condemns? Christ Jesus . . . is interceding for us." (v. 34). "Who shall separate us from the love of Christ?" (v. 35).

When that service ended, I quietly slipped away to my study, and God gave me an experience/insight of the heart. I was reminded that, when life throws me those hardballs that knock the emotional wind out of me, I need to totally acknowledge that God is my strength.

*Encouragement from Scripture*

What, then, shall we say in response to this? If God is for us, who can be against us? He who did not spare his own Son, but gave him up for us all—how will he not also, along with him, graciously give us all things? Who will bring any charge against those whom God has chosen? It is God who justifies. Who is he that condemns? Christ Jesus, who died—more than that, who was raised to life—is at the right hand of God and is also interceding for us. Who shall separate us from the love of Christ? (Romans 8:31-35)

What has been my experience at being more than a conqueror as a result of God's power and love? Today I will remember that I grow stronger one day at a time and I will remember that healing takes time—lots of time.

*My prayer*

Give me courage and strength to withstand whatever comes into my life today.

*Now I will take some moments to rest with God.*

*My spiritual healing journal*

Date     Thoughts / Feelings / Insight Gained / Prayer

_____

_____

_____

_____

_____

# 8 Today with God's help: I will let God give me victory over depression

*Encouragement from experience*

Power thoughts: The Scripture tells us that greater is the one that is in us than the one that is in the world. (See John 16.) Victory over discouragement and depression is before you; reach out to God and to at least one other person to give that victory.

Depression can turn your life upside down with the swing of a mood. Experts tell us that depression involves what's going on inside of us as well as what's happening outside of us. Chemical imbalances in the brain can cause depression. Life events—such as the death of a loved one, relationship problems, a job loss, a difficult transition, and even the birth of a baby—can trigger depression. Sometimes certain drugs or combinations of drugs can bring on depression. When life throws you a hardball of depression, reach out for help. Help from God, help from friends, help from the Scriptures, help from your physician or pastor. Take tiny steps toward healing. As you begin to take action and make choices, even small ones, you will start to feel less hopelessness, and you will be more able to cope. Break large, overwhelming tasks into smaller manageable ones. Be patient with yourself.

*Encouragement from Scripture*

What, then, shall we say in response to this? And our response can be, "If God is for us, who can be against us?" (Romans 8:31)

Let your gentleness be evident to all. The Lord is near. Do not be anxious about anything, but in everything, by prayer and petition, with thanksgiving, present your requests to God. (Philippians 4:5-6)

*My response as I claim God's promises and grow stronger*

How has depression affected my life, and what steps will I take to gain victory?

*Practical steps that I will take today*

Today I will remember that every day is a new gift from God. I will remember that I can learn from mistakes that others and I may have made. I will reflect on God's blessings. I will remember that healing takes time—lots of time.

*My prayer*

Grant me victory today in overcoming any depression that I may feel.

*Now I will take some moments to rest with God.*

*My spiritual healing journal*

Date      Thoughts / Feelings / Insight Gained / Prayer

_____

_____

_____

_____

_____

# Resources

### Alzheimer's

Alzheimer's Association. *URL:* http://www.alz.org. *Email:* info@ alz.org. *Address:* 919 North Michigan Avenue, Suite 1000, Chicago, IL 60611-1676. *Phone:* 1-800-272-3900. Chicago-based volunteer group that provides caregiver resources, chapter locations, and treatment and research information.

### Anxiety

Anxiety Disorders Association of America. *URL:* http://www .adaa.org. *Address:* 8730 Georgia Avenue, Suite 600, Silver Spring, MD 20910. *Phone:* 1-240-485-1001. Peruse resources on various forms of anxiety conditions, or browse comments on the message board. Includes research information for professionals.

### Bereaved

Bereaved Parents of the USA. *URL:* http://www.bereaved parentsusa.org. *Address:* National Office, P.O. Box 95, Park Forest, IL 60466. *Phone:* 1-708-748-7866. Nationwide network that organizes meetings for parents, grandparents, and siblings of a deceased child. Visit the section for the newly bereaved.

Beyond Indigo: Changing the Way You Feel about Grief and Loss. *URL:* http://www.beyondindigo.com. Send a question to a grief expert, read over past newsletters, discuss terminal illness and legal issues, and visit the section for teens.

The Compassionate Friends National Headquarters. *URL:* http://www.compassionatefriends.org. *Address:* P.O. Box

3696, Oak Brook, IL 60522-3696. *Phone:* 1-877-969-0010 or 1-630-990-0010. Healing from the death of a child—all ages.

Dougy Center: The National Center for Grieving Children and Families. *URL:* http://www.dougy.org. *Email:* help@dougy.org. *Address:* 3909 S.E. 52nd Avenue, P.O. Box 86852, Portland, OR 97286. *Phone:* 1-503-775-5683.

Elisabeth Kübler-Ross Center. *URL:* http://www.elisabeth kublerross.com. *Address:* South Route 616, Head Waters, VA 24442. *Phone:* 1-703-396-3441.

Grief and Loss—American Association of Retired Persons. *URL:* http://www.griefandloss.org. *Address:* 601 E. Street N.W., Washington, DC 20049. *Phone:* 1-888-687-2277. AARP offers resources to help individuals and families grieve the loss of a loved one, such as a child, spouse, sibling, or parent. Find articles and advice.

Make Today Count. *URL:* http://www.smsu.edu/nursing/ community/Agency_folder/MakeTodayCount.htm. *Address:* 1235 E. Cherokee, Springfield MO 65804-2263. *Phone:* 1-800-432-2273 or 1-417-885-3324. Offers emotional support to people who are experiencing grief or loss. Make Today Count, Inc., is a nationwide support organization for all persons affected by cancer or other life-threatening illness; patients, families, healthcare professionals, and interested persons.

Tischler, Janet. Perinatal Bereavement Consultant. *Address:* 16 Cresent Drive, Parsippany, NM 07054-1605. *Phone:* 1-201-966-6437. Healing from losses due to miscarriage, infant death, or stillbirth.

*Books for Children (Ages 3–7)*

Buscaglia, Leo. *Freddie the Leaf.* New York: Holt, Rinehart, and Winston, 1982.

Harris, Audrey. *Why Did He Die?* Minneapolis: Lerner Publications, 1965.

Stein, Sarah B. *About Dying*. New York: Walker and Company, 1974.

Viorst, Judith. *The Tenth Good Thing about Barney*. New York: Atheneum, 1972.

### Books for Children (Ages 8–14)

Corley, Elizabeth. *Tell Me About Death, Tell Me About Funerals.* Santa Clara, CA.: Grammatical Sciences, 1973.

Fassler, Joan. *My Grandpa Died Today.* New York: Behavioral Publications, 1971.

L'Engle, Madeleine. *A Ring of Endless Light.* New York: Farrar, Straus, Giroux, 1980.

LeShan, Eda. *Learning to Say Good-Bye.* New York: Macmillan Publishing, 1972.

See also below: *Sudden Infant Death Syndrome*

### Caregiving

*American College of Physicians Home Care Guide. URL:* http://www.acponline.org/public/h_care. Offers an outline for cancerous and life-limited people. Practical advice for caretakers as well as for the ones who are facing death.

Children of Aging Parents. *URL:* http://www.caps4caregivers .org. *Address:* P.O. Box 167, Richboro, PA 18954, *Phone:* 1-800-227-7294. Provides referrals for attorneys, retirement communities, medical insurance, and respite care. Learn about educational outreach efforts.

St. Francis Center. *Address:* 5135 MacArther Boulevard N.W., Washington, DC 20016. *Phone:* 1-202-363-8500. Provides counseling and support groups, HIV/AIDS program, children and adolescent program.

Christianity.com. *URL:* http://christianity.com. They sponsor Christianity Online chat room (*URL:* http://forums.christianity .com), which has lots of information. Please note: chat rooms have advantages and disadvantages and this is not an unqualified endorsement.

Church Central. *URL:* http://churchcentral.com. At the heart of church health and leadership, providing pastors, denominational executives, and paraministry leaders with valuable news and advice.

Glorieta Conference Center. *Address:* P.O. Box 8, Glorieta, NM 87535-0008.

LifeWay Christian Resources. *URL:* http://www.lifeway.com. *Address:* International Headquarters, One LifeWay Plaza, Nashville, TN 37234. Offers Christian resources for teachers, pastors, church staff, ministry leaders, and church members.

Ridgecrest Conference Center. *Address:* P.O. Box 128, Ridgecrest, NC 28770.

711 Christian Search. *URL:* http://search.711.net. *Email:* admin@ 711.net. *Address:* 2063 N Lecanto Hwy., Lecanto, FL 34461. *Phone:* 1-866-558-6778.

United States Conference of Catholic Bishops. *URL:* http:// www.usccb.org. *Address:* 3211 Fourth Street N.E., Washington, DC 20017. *Phone:* 1-202-541-3000. News and information from the official Catholic resource in the United States.

*Depression*

About Depression. *URL:* http://depression.about.com. Find practical details about living with depression. Includes advice on depression disorders and treatment, on suicide, and on seeking help.

American Society of Clinical Psychopharmacology. *Address:* P.O. Box 40395, Glen Oaks, NY 11004. *Phone:* 1-718-470-4007.

National Foundation for Depressive Illness. *URL:* http://www .depression.org. Aims to educate the public about depressive illness. Browse the list of common symptoms or check out tips to help combat depression.

### Divorce

Fresh Start Seminars. *URL:* http://www.freshstartseminars .org. *Address:*1440 Russell Road Paoli, PA 19301. *Phone:* 1-888-373-7478 or 1-610-644-4066. Christian group provides seminars and support groups for adults and children dealing with divorce. Find a discussion forum and an event schedule.

NCH—It's Not Your Fault. *URL:* http://www.itsnotyourfault.org. Provides resources for kids, teens, and parents for dealing with divorce. Participate in the survey.

### Domestic Violence

American Bar Association. *URL:* http://www.abanet.org/domviol/ home.html. *Address:* 740 15th Street N.W., 9th Floor, Washington, DC 20005-1022. Information that includes links to shelters and support groups. For help call the National Domestic Violence Hotline: 1-800-799-7233 or 1-800-787-3224 (TTY).

National Domestic Violence Hotline. *URL:* http://www.ndvh.org. Help and information. "If you need help call us right now! 1-800-799-7233 or 1-800-787-3224." Offers shelter referrals and safety tips.

### Funeral Planning

Curley, Terence P. *Planning the Catholic Funeral.* Collegeville, MN: Liturgical Press, 2005.

Federal Trade Commission. *Funerals: A Consumer Guide. URL:* http://www.ftc.gov/bcp/conline/pubs/services/funeral.htm. Contains advice for consumers on funeral costs and industry rules.

FuneralPlan.com. *URL:* http://funeralplan.com. Offers advice on all aspects of funeral planning from making a will to choosing a type of ceremony.

## Hospice

American Hospice Foundation. *URL:* http://www.american hospice.org. *Email:* ahf@americanhospice.org. *Address:* 2120 L Street N.W., Suite 200, Washington, DC 20037. *Phone:* 202-223-0204. Dedicated to caring for those where cure is no longer possible. Find publications, training workshops, and a hospice directory.

Hospice Association of America. *URL:* http://www.nahc.org. Offers guidelines and resources for the hospice industry. Find consumer information, education opportunities, and news.

## Insurance

Standard Publishing Corp. *URL:* http://www.standardpublishing corp.com. *Address:* 155 Federal Street, 13th Floor, Boston, MA 02110. *Phone:* 617-457-0600. An insurance resource: aspects of property/casualty insurance, risk management, and workers' compensation.

## Life Issues

Right to Life—USA. *URL:* http://www.nrlc.org. National organization opposed to abortion and euthanasia. Site includes information, alerts, abortion alternatives, and news.

## Publishers

Augsburg Fortress. *URL:* http://www.augsburgfortress.org. *Address:* P.O. Box 1209, Minneapolis, MN 55440-1209. *Phone:* 1-800-328-4648 (U.S.) or 1-800- 265-6397. A publishing house run by the Evangelical Lutheran Church in America.

Cook Communications Ministries. *URL:* http://www.cook ministries.com. *Address:* 4050 Lee Vance View. Colorado Springs, CO 80918. *Phone:* 1-800-708-5550 or 719-536-0100. Provides books, journals, and other resources for Christian spiritual growth. Includes a forum for discussion of experiences.

GospelLight.com. *URL:* http://www.gospellight.com. Christian books, children's and youth ministry.

Group Publishing. *URL:* http://www.grouppublishing.com. *Email:* info@group.com. *Address:* P.O. Box 481, Loveland, CO 80539. *Phone:* 1-800-447-1070. Christian publisher offers magazines, books, and resources for ministers and Christian educators. Includes training and seminars.

Judson Press. *URL:* http://www.judsonpress.com. *Address:* American Baptist Churches in the USA, P.O. Box 851, Valley Forge, PA 19482-0851. *Phone:* 1 800-222-3872 or 1-610-768-2000. The publishing arm of American Baptist Churches in the U.S.A., an evangelical, ecumenical, interracial denomination with a global outreach.

Liturgical Press. *URL:* http://www.litpress.org. *Email:* sales@ litpress.org. *Address:* Saint John's Abbey, P.O. Box 7500, Collegeville, MN 56321-7500. *Phone:* 1-800-858-5450 or 1-800-363-2213. Publisher of *Healing Takes Time*. Publishes numerous resources in spirituality, theology, liturgy, and preaching.

Serendipity House. *URL:* http://www.serendipityhouse.com. "On this web site you will find everything you need to know about Serendipity and how we can help your small group ministry." *Email:* debra.hinkle@serendipityhouse.com. *Address:* 117 10th Avenue N., Nashville, TN 37234. *Phone:* 1-800-525-9563.

Stephen Ministries. *URL:* http://www.stephenministries.org. *Address:* 2045 Innerbelt Business Center Dr., St. Louis, MO 63114-5765. *Phone:* 1-314-428-2600. "A transdenominational Christian education organization that provides high quality training and resources to strengthen and expand lay ministry in congregations."

Stretcher Bearers for Christ. *URL:* http://www.stretcher bearers.com. The website of Stretcher Bearers for Christ is dedicated to helping lost souls find their way. Peter and Rebekah Laue, 965 Cloud Cap Avenue, Pagosa Springs, CO 81147.

### Sudden Infant Death Syndrome

American Sudden Infant Death Syndrome Institute. *URL:* http://www.sids.org. *Address:* 6560 Roswell Road, Suite 876, Atlanta, GA 30328. *Phone:* 1-800-232-7437 or 770-426-8746.

CJ Foundation for SIDS. *URL:* http://www.cjsids.com. The Don Imus-WFAN Pediatric Center, Hackensack University Medical Center, 30 Prospect Avenue, Hackensack, NJ 07601. *Phone:* 1-888-825-7437 or 1-201-996-5111. A nationwide, voluntary health organization that funds research and community support services.

Federal SIDS Program. *Address:* Office of Maternal and Child Health, Bureau of Maternal and Child Health and Resources Development, Parklawn Building, Room 9–31, 5600 Fishers Lane, Rockville, MD 20857.

National Center for the Prevention of Sudden Infant Death Syndrome. *Address:* 330 North Charles Street, Baltimore, MD 21201. *Phone:* 1-800-638-7437.

National SIDS Resource Center. *URL:* http://www.sidscenter .org. *Address:* 8201 Greensboro Drive, Suite 600, McLean, VA 22102. *Phone:* 1-703-821-8955. On the website find an outline of NSRC products and services, an introduction to SIDS, and resource links.

National Sudden Infant Death Syndrome Foundation. *Address:* 10500 Little Patuxent Parkway, Suite 420, Columbia, MD 21044. *Phone:* 1-800-221-7437.